Climbing
Anchors

HOW TO CLIMB™ SERIES

Climbing Anchors

Second Edition

JOHN LONG and BOB GAINES

FALCON GUIDES ®

GUILFORD, CONNECTICUT
HELENA, MONTANA

AN IMPRINT OF THE GLOBE PEQUOT PRESS

FALCONGUIDES®

Text copyright © 2006 John Long and Bob Gaines
Portions of this book were previously published in *Climbing Anchors* by John Long
(Chockstone Press, Inc., 1993) and *More Climbing Anchors* by John Long and Bob
Gaines (Chockstone Press, Inc., reprinted by Falcon Publishing, Inc., 1996).

Photos © Bob Gaines unless noted otherwise
Section opener spot photos by photos.com
Illustrations © Mike Clelland

Library of Congress Cataloging-in-Publication Data
Long, John, 1953-
 Climbing anchors / John Long and Bob Gaines. — 2nd ed.
  p. cm.
 Originally published: Evergreen, Colo. : Chockstone Press, 1993.
 ISBN-13: 978-0-7627-2326-3
 1. Rock climbing—Equipment and supplies. 2. Rock climbing—Safety
measures. I. Gaines, Bob, 1959- . II. Title.
GV200.15.L66 2006
796.52′2—dc22

                   2006009207

Printed in the United States of America
Second Edition/Third Printing

"Whenever building any anchor, *everything* (be it a 4-foot-thick tree or a shiny new bolt) deserves a second thought."

—From a thread on *rockclimbing.com*

Contents

Acknowledgments

Special thanks to Jim Ewing, research and development manager at Sterling Ropes, who conducted all the drop tests; Mark Chatwin, of Chatwin Guides, and Kolin Powick, quality assurance manager at Black Diamond, who critiqued versions of the text; Tom Cecil, of Seneca Rocks Mountain Guides, who exhaustively field-tested rigging systems; Dr. Richard Goldstone and Craig Connally, who provided studied opinions and hard figures about fall forces and anchor systems; Dr. Lawrence Hamilton and Dr. Callie Rennison, who fashioned the statistical analysis for Jim's testing; editor and project expediter John Burbidge, who kept this monster on course from start to finish; and my co-author, Bob Gaines, director of Vertical Adventures, who—among many other duties—provided most of the photos.

Liz Dunn-Tierney on *Rock Lobster*, Otter Cliff, Acadia National Park, Maine. PHOTO BY STEWART M. GREEN.

Introduction

When we first wrote *Climbing Anchors* and *More Climbing Anchors,* our aim was to try and standardize the entire subject into basic components and protocols generic enough they would apply to everything from the sandstone desert bluffs of Moab, to the great granite walls of Yosemite. It's remarkable to think that just a decade ago there were few common terms (most of which I either made up or filched from different sources) for even the most basic elements of an anchor, and there were even fewer standard protocols about how to build them. We venture into this new edition with most of the terms now known and used by all and with the basic protocols established and refined by millions of climbers in many lands.

And yet in some ways this book is far trickier to put together than when I wrote the first anchor book in 1992. Over the last dozen or so years, the strengths and weaknesses of the basic systems have been examined 1,001 times. The short-form verdict is that the majority of our anchoring techniques are provisional, not absolute. Furthermore there are often trade-offs in choosing one technique over another. Lastly, while we'd like each anchor to conform to a wide-ranging evalua-tion criteria called SRENE (solid, redundant, equalized and no extension), it's the rare anchor that can accomplish this even close to 100 percent. If we could sug-gest a few protocols that would absolutely work in absolutely every situation, I could write this book in fifty pages. Instead it will take us four times as long to grasp an exceedingly fluid subject. Climbing anchors are largely a matter of com-promises; the trick is developing a feel for what you should and should not com-promise at a given place on the rock.

For several reasons we've decided to load *Climbing Anchors* and *More Climbing Anchors* into one volume to provide a single Anchor Omnibus. As climbing has con-tinued to grow over the last ten years, trends have evolved and gear has changed. In the meantime the Internet has taken over the universe. On countless threads on countless climbing Web sites, anchors have remained a hotly debated topic, pro-viding invaluable perspectives drawn from real, on-the-rock experiences. Reader feedback and Web dialogues, along with a growing (but incomplete) database of lab-derived facts and figures, have led to such a thorough reworking of our original material that little beyond the basic breakdowns and a few photos survive in the present edition.

That much said, the task of compiling a definitive text on anchors will always be lacking because of the inexhaustible variables found on the rock. There are also dozens of methods and as many ideas about how to execute most all the basic anchoring procedures. If we were to include even a fraction of these, this book would run a thousand pages long. While the material in this book is, strictly speaking, nothing more than our experiential opinion about a broad-reaching subject, that opinion has drawn heavily from manufacturers, instructors, guides and leading climbers in the United States and beyond. Heeding current refinements and wrangling it all into one standardized *modus operandi* is the mission of this book. And the starting point for all of this is the philosophy underlying the entire subject of climbing anchors.

THE SOURCES

Hard information about anchors and protection are drawn from two sources: the lab and the field. Lab testing provides facts, figures and general counsel per the specs of this material and that system. Using the collected knowledge of physics and engineering, along with evolving testing methods and computer analysis, lab tests yield crucial generic information.

Climbing is not a lab job, however, so we cannot expect lab tests to furnish protocols applicable directly and infallibly to actual climbing scenarios. Sometimes they do, but field testing ultimately determines if a lab-hatched technique lives or dies. Conversely, techniques and methods drawn from the field are frequently lab tested in the hopes of isolating the pros and cons of a given technique, system or particular piece of gear. If we've learned anything over the last twenty years, it's that the limitless variety of geology will always frustrate a one-size-fits-all anchor strategy. Manufacturer catalogs and Web sites offer illustrated ways to do most everything, rarely mentioning that there are times when you *cannot* do things as advertised. Again, more than simply showing you what to do, this book concentrates on developing an understanding of basic principles so thoroughly that with time and experience, you can decide for yourself what to do.

Conveying this information in a book presents several challenges. Our method is to cover the material in both theoretical and practical terms. Once the theory is covered in the text (and summarized in multiple sidebars), we place the reader, via illustrations and photographs, in a real world climbing situation and ask: "What might we do here?" Then we proceed to show concrete options, giving pros and cons for each.

A change in this volume is that "What might we do here?" is largely spelled out through applying a general principle to a specific set of circumstances. The photos will typically illustrate a concept (such as equalization, redundancy, etc.), with the

Peter Croft leading *Astroturf,* Joshua Tree, California. PHOTO BY BOB GAINES.

photos grouped to show the concepts applied in various ways. By seeing a concept
come to life in a dihedral, under a roof, or in a horizontal crack, we learn to diversify
our basic toolkit, while coming to appreciate that we can never eliminate judgment
and creativity from the art of building anchors. Once you are out on the cliff, you
have to work with what you have on your rack and what the rock affords. It is debatable whether there is ever some objective "best way" to build an anchor at a given
location. Every anchor is a matter of compromises. We compromise our desire for
anchor overkill by placing two instead of six bolts at a belay station; in the name of
proficiency we build a hanging belay from five, not fifteen, nuts, and so on.

SECURE

This leads to the great conundrum about the entire topic of anchors: What does "secure" actually mean? Or more accurately, what *should* "secure" mean? Not in a theoretical sense, but in the sense in which a real climber will confront a real situation on a real rock and must make decisions that will keep her alive. Without "cliff sense" and acceptance that skilled climbing is efficient climbing, some people consider the subject in terms of absolutes. "Secure" will then be defined and defended from a position of neurotic fear, resulting in needless overkill in the quest to achieve the impossible goal of absolute safety. Such thinking, if applied to freeway driving, would lead us all to rumble down the road in Abrams tanks. But it's impractical to do so, so most of us are fine with driving a car with some—though not absolute—protective qualities. Yet as any experienced driver will tell you, the key to avoiding accidents is not to drive a tank, but to stay on the ball and avoid risky maneuvers.

Hidetaka Suzuki finger jamming on *The Phoenix*, Yosemite, California. PHOTO BY BOB GAINES.

Instead of improving one's wherewithal on the cliff side, gym-trained sport-climbing has introduced a brand of climber prone to believe safety comes from the equipment and the systems themselves, instead of how these are used. This expectation can never be realized in the field. Secure climbing remains the product of experience, knowledge, judgment and common sense, as opposed to the gear you employ. Our gear and our methods must be "good enough," but unless we can accept that "good enough" can never be an absolute, we'll keep looking for the climbing equivalent of that Abrams tank. Not only will we never find it, we'll waste everyone's time overbuilding anchors and exasperating our partners with specious arguments chasing the unreachable goal of total safety.

In practical terms, "better" means "stronger" only if what you have is not "strong enough." Allow me an example. Several years ago a group of us met at a local beachside crag, rotating between slab climbing and body surfing throughout the morning. Around noon we decided to step it up and string a toprope over a vertical 80-foot seaside cliff sporting some challenging face routes. I rigged the TR with a 50-foot loop of static cord clipped to half a dozen bolts on top. I draped the anchor line over the lip, which I'd padded with a pack, and, via two locking biners, gates opposed, connected the climbing rope to a double figure eight knot tied in the static line, thus creating my "power point." Just to be sure, and because I could rig it in ten seconds flat, I backed up the static line with a runner clipped off to three topside bolts. You could have tethered a submarine off this anchor, but for one guy it wasn't "good enough." He wanted me to tie another power point, just in case the one already doubled power point should fail, along with the back-up runner. He kept on about how much "safer" his method was, as opposed to what we'd rigged. It was a little like trying to argue with someone terrified of butterflies. You get nowhere, no matter how rational your arguments.

> **Remember . . .**
>
> - A stronger belay anchor is not necessarily a better anchor.
>
> - Climbing gear rarely breaks, but it often pulls out.
>
> - Even the strongest primary placements are worthless unless they are *securely unified into the roped safety system.*
>
> - Protection and the belay anchor work in tandem with judgment, experience and belaying and climbing skill.

Here we have someone trying to judge an anchor by absolutes. His method would have provided a stronger anchor, but not one any more secure since what we had was easily ten times as strong as was needed for toproping. In any practical sense, his idealized anchor was a bust—and he never forgave me for not rigging it out to his phobic specs. An hour later, we'd all run multiple laps on the steep face and the fellow was still carping about the sketchy anchor, a self-inflicted martyr of all-or-nothing thinking.

WHEN DOES "GOOD ENOUGH" BECOME TOO MUCH?

"Good enough" does not mean barely enough to keep you from dying. Good enough means an anchor that will unquestionably hold the greatest forces a climbing team can place upon it. Additionally, every experienced climber factors in a safety margin of at least one fold, meaning the anchor is built to withstand at least twice as much impact as that generated by a factor 2 fall (explained later). "Good enough" does not mean an anchor capable of holding a celestial body, which has forces you can never generate on a rock climb. An anchor that can hold Neptune in orbit is not "better" than a "good-enough" anchor because the former is safeguarding against purely imaginary forces. And we should know that even this advice is impossible to follow at least some of the time. It's likely that at some point you will find yourself hanging from anchors you pray to God are good enough, while knowing that they are probably not. Once you start up a rock wall, there are no guarantees.

In short, this manual is geared to provide tangible, specific, comprehensive and user-friendly information to climbers who are learning how to place protection, and who arrive at the end of a pitch and have to construct an anchor to safeguard their lives. As Canadian big-wall icon Hugh Burton stated, "Without a bombproof anchor you have nothing." The importance of sound anchors cannot be overstated.

That much said, protection and the belay anchor are only parts of a hazard-mitigating system that works in tandem with judgment, experience and belaying and climbing skill to protect the team from the potential dangers of falling. Here risk evaluation can only be broached in terms of placements (protection or "pro") and anchors; the rest falls under leading skills, which is a separate study imperative for all aspiring climbers.

BASIC ANCHOR BUILDING FACTS:

- "Perfect" rarely exists in real world climbing anchors.
- No single rigging technique will work in every situation.
- Trad climbers must efficiently improvise on a handful of anchor building techniques.
- The ability to improvise requires a thorough understanding of basic principles.
- Climbing anchors always involve compromises—the trick is to understand what you should and should not compromise at a given place on the rock.

MODERN RIGGING METHODS ARE NO SILVER BULLET

Over the last twenty years ingenious rigging methods have been developed, methods that were much needed and long overdue. These methods, described throughout this book, take practice to master, though mastering them ensures nothing. In some cases climbers have come to put more emphasis on these rigging methods—the way in which they combine various components of an anchor matrix—than on the security and holding strength of the components themselves. Simply stated, the purpose of modern rigging methods is to exploit every possible ounce of holding strength from a given anchor in order to make it secure. But believe it: All the fancy rigging in the world cannot compensate for individual nuts, pitons, cams and bolts that themselves are unsound.

Consider, for example, an interesting experiment we ran some years ago at Trash Can Rock, out at Joshua Tree National Monument. Someone had an old VW Bug, and we got the crazy idea of testing anchors built in the nearby cracks by hooking up a line to the chassis of the Bug and loading the anchors till the Bug's tires spun in the gravel or the anchor shot from the nearby wall. We broke several biners and slings, mangled a few spring-loaded camming devices (SLCDs) and hexes, and in the process learned to take cover when the Bug went into gear and the anchors were "tested."

Though this exercise would never qualify as proper science, it did indicate the absolute holding power of a given primary anchor and various rigging systems. By a ratio of about 10 to 1, the anchors that held the Bug fast consisted of large passive nuts lodged in bottleneck placements and rigged with the most rudimentary tie-in systems. Elaborate and ornate anchors consisting of five or more small-to-medium-sized devices, ingeniously equalized and built to absolutely perfect, textbook specs, were always the first ones to fail. Basic, bombproof nuts simply rigged proved time and again to be the anchors that provided the most security.

Before we get into the instructional part of the text, it's worth touching on some recent tragedies involving anchor failure with the intention of avoiding the same mistakes. Without getting too technical, recent anchor failures suggest that the most vulnerable setups tend to be combinations of small to medium nuts and cams placed in horizontal cracks, rigged with elaborate equalization systems. This is not to say bomber anchors cannot be obtained with small nuts in horizontal cracks, rather that when building such anchors, special care is required to make sure the anchor is indeed "good enough." Moreover we must wonder if the victims of these anchor failures (all fatal) believed that the modern rigging methods would automatically transform a poor anchor—in terms of primary placements—into a good one. We can never know the answer to this question, but it's one we should never lose sight of.

The lesson here, and one fundamental to this manual, is that the starting point of any anchor is setting bombproof primary placements. The means by which you connect the various components into an anchor matrix should never be relied upon to provide the needed strength not found in the primary, individual placements. Furthermore, the goal is not simply strength, but security. More on this later.

SRENE—SOUND PRACTICE, BUT NOT THE FINAL WORD IN ANCHORS

When I wrote out the "rules" in my previous two anchor books, the idea was to establish general protocols that would maximize the likelihood of folks building failsafe anchors. Over a short time the rules got codified into a sort of gospel—by no means my own, since I drew upon many sources (including Marc Chauvin and the American Mountain Guides Association)—and after standardizing the terminology, I wove the lot into one overall strategy. Perhaps the result saved a few lives.

The downside of this "gospel" is twofold: First, folks came to believe that if the anchor met the SRENE (solid, redundant, equalized and no extension) criteria, then it was automatically secure and fail-safe. Second, any anchor that did not meet the criteria was, without exception, a liability, as was the climber who placed it. Reality does not support either notion. There are far too many accounts of well-rigged anchors that failed for the simple reason that SRENE criteria cannot compensate for bad primary placements (again, bombproof placements remain the backbone of all sound anchors).

The fact is, even SRENE criteria cannot be met in absolute terms. No anchor is ever perfectly equalized; a well-equalized anchor commonly has some possibility of "extension" if one component in the anchor matrix fails; and few anchors feature textbook redundancy. The true value of SRENE is for use as an evaluation strategy, not as some ideal anchoring model you can and should attain. But even if someone, somewhere *could* build perfect, SRENE anchors, we could never apply the criteria across the board and believe we had the danger licked. Though I would not recommend anyone violating the SRENE code, there are anchors out there that do not conform to SRENE, and yet these anchors are literally capable of holding a car.

KEY SRENE POINTS

SRENE is an evaluation strategy, not a checklist.

Observance of every SRENE principle does not guarantee that an anchor will hold a single pound.

Modern rigging techniques cannot compensate for insecure primary placements.

With strong primary placements and modern rigging techniques providing security, climbing's roped safety system is typically very reliable.

THE MODERN CLIMBER VS. THE YOSEMITE PIONEERS

Newsweek recently reported that there are 1.9 million active rock climbers in the United States. "Active" was broadly defined, and the 1.9 million figure was probably cooked by the gear trade. But go to any popular gym or sport-climbing area and you'll see a regular ant farm teeming over the holds, so perhaps *Newsweek*'s estimate was not so far off.

Thirty years ago, Bill Forrest—an innovator of modern climbing equipment—used to travel the country hawking harnesses, copperheads and plastic nuts off the ass-end of his pickup. Nowadays, annual sales of climbing gear run in the hundreds of millions of dollars. Space-age materials, computer modeling and ingenious designs provide excellent protection devices. Likewise, anchoring methods and rigging systems have become a special study. Still, with all this technology thrown at what twenty-five years ago was a niche sport, you'd think rock climbing would be less dangerous than ever before—but statistics indicate that the injury per climber ratio has actually increased over the last few decades. Why? The answer can never be fully known, but I believe two main reasons stand out. Both are crucial to understand as they drive the basic philosophy of this manual.

The first reason is obvious. The bulk of present-day climbers learned the ropes in a climbing gym, not on the rock. In a gym, the anchors and protection are fixed in place and bombproof, so a belayer and a leader need only know basic clipping, belaying and lowering techniques to keep the game adequately secure. That frees up a gym climber to concentrate on the physical moves, and the learning curve is quick for most anyone fit and motivated.

The problem comes after a gym climber acquires blazing licks on plastic, and expects that prowess to translate directly to the outdoors. This often proves so, to greater or lesser degrees, on the limited venue of clip-and-go sport routes, where every bolt is fixed and the routes rarely top 100 feet. But consider traditional (trad) climbing. Here a leader must place most if not all the protection and build anchors, often complicated ones, as well as rig and perform multiple rappels, on routes upwards of 3,000 feet long. Anyone can appreciate that the gym provides little preparation for such serious adventures.

In the old pre-gym era, from day one climbers were obliged to set anchors and protection, as well as rig and perform rappels. The downside of the old-school curriculum was that it often took several seasons for an active climber to start leading routes approaching the 5.9 grade, something most gym climbers now achieve in weeks, if not days or even hours. The upside was that from the outset climbers of old gained experience with, and a practical grasp of, both the gear and how to use it, while slowly developing a comfort zone on the rock. The result was far fewer basic mistakes and fewer accidents than those suffered, per capita, by present-day climbers.

The second reason that modern gear and techniques have not by themselves reduced the danger quotient is more difficult to explain and understand. Basically, much of the modern testing has focused on calculating the breaking point of ropes, slings, "high-tensile cord" and every piece of hardware ever made. Because these items are generally more robust than is required in the field, the high test

Sandy Litchfield on *#1 Super Guy,* Shelf Road, Colorado. PHOTO BY STEWART M. GREEN.

scores might be great as a sales tool, but they add little *new* information to our study of anchoring systems. More apropos is when the engineers strength-test methods of securing the anchors—alone, and in groups or matrixes—to the climbing rope. Rigging, in other words. Before about 1975, there wasn't much strategy about how to rig an anchor beyond trying to snug the knots up so the forces of a fall (the actual figures were then largely unknown) would be somewhat displaced between the various pieces of the anchor matrix. In the old school, the main emphasis was on the strength of the anchors themselves—the primary placements—not on how you connected or equalized them. The thinking was: build an anchor from individual placements that are absolutely bombproof, impossible to pull out "no matter what." Then tie the thing off, snug up those knots and get on with it.

By most criteria, if you were to replicate the anchors used by the Yosemite pioneers on the first ascent of virtually every big wall, they would be deemed unsatisfactory, owing to the ways in which the individual placements were rigged together. But statistics do not bear out this appraisal for one irrefutable reason: None of the old pioneers, or any of their immediate followers, ever died from anchor failure.

A SHIFT IN PRIORITIES

Fast forward to forty years later. A bunch of folks start casually testing new ways to rig anchors and, after field input and tweaking, those ways become standardized, as well they should have. Without anyone taking note, there is a subtle shift in priorities, from the primacy of the basic anchor points, the individual nuts, bolts, pitons, etc., to the way these anchor points are joined together. The new rigging strategies furnished significant advances, rendering much more secure anchors for the same placements of the old timers. But as new rigging configurations became standard practice across America, perhaps too much emphasis came to be placed on the setups, while in some cases the importance of the primary anchor points became secondary. As we've already touched upon, and will keep touching upon, some climbers came to believe that the new rigging systems were so great that any old anchor would do, so long as it was rigged according to SRENE criteria. Climbers of old, on the other hand, had little concept of SRENE, and instead put their confidence in the outright holding strength of the individual placements, content to bash home enough pitons so that the anchor would hold "no matter what."

But these pioneers had the luxury of acquiring monumentally strong anchors with steel pitons 95 percent of the time. Nobody's arguing in favor of bringing back the piton for security's sake—the rock suffered too much damage. Still it's taken us roughly forty years to develop passive gear and rigging systems that can now approximate the brute strength attained by the pioneers with their racks of chrome molly steel. And yet anchor failure has become a more common occurrence. Hence, the need for this manual.

ABOUT THIS BOOK

The mission of this book is to provide the following:

- A simple, basic philosophy that guides the entire process
- A set of general, tangible motifs and rules-of-thumb to focus the overall process
- The general themes clarified through text, sidebars and specific examples via pictures, illustrations and breakdowns

Practical value is the guiding principle of this manual. There's no getting around the fact that this is a textbook, technical by nature. I'm not writing it for fun or amusement (though I hope some might find parts of the text amusing), and my impulse to make it flow like a short story has been sacrificed in an effort toward thoroughness. The sheer volume of information can sometimes overwhelm the beginner. Although the many sidebars break down each key topic into simple bullet points, there's still no getting around doing some heavy lifting to get through the material, especially if the subject is somewhat new to you.

Before you get involved in the specifics, though, always keep in mind two basic principles we will elaborate on throughout this book. First, the primary concern in building secure anchors must be the outright holding power of the individual placements themselves. Second, the means by which the individual anchors are linked together into an anchor matrix should always take into account modern rigging protocols and criteria, with the emphasis being on simplicity and efficiency. By keeping these two cardinal rules in our head, the sometimes-confusing configurations and infinite options of building anchors can be made much more straightforward.

There are many topics more involved and complex than climbing anchors, but few where the concepts are so rigorously applied, and where slipshod workmanship can so quickly make you dead. This is the main reason to take your time with this material. We've all crammed for exams, then later walked from the classroom with all that we "knew" pouring from our beans like flour from a sieve. The material herein can never be absolutely mastered. Once you absorb the basic concepts, it comes down to experience and judgment, qualities that come in their own time—or not. Rock climbing is not for everyone, especially adventure or "trad" climbing, for which this book is especially germane. Building anchors is a lifelong study, so pace yourself, and live long.

WHEN BUILDING ANCHORS, ALWAYS REMEMBER . . .

- The primary concern must be the outright holding power of the individual placements.
- Use modern rigging methods and criteria to link the individual placements.
- Slipshod workmanship can kill you.
- Double-check your work and your partner's.
- Building anchors is a lifelong study.

A BRIEF HISTORY OF ROCK HARDWARE

If a modern-day rock climber could time-travel back forty years to the halcyon days in Yosemite, she would see equipment and techniques that few remember and fewer still ever used. Back then, boots, or Kletterschues, were more like clodhoppers, with their stiff uppers and rock-hard cleated soles. Ropes were adequate, but not nearly as versatile and durable as the modern article. Protecting the lead was a business of slugging home pitons and slinging the odd horn. Artificial chockstones (nuts) were available, but most were weird, funky widgets with limited utility. Save for really bombproof placements, these first nuts were far less reliable than pitons for securing the rope to the cliff.

In 1970 most nuts were European imports. The best came from England, where they were invented. Initially American climbers were suspicious of nuts, and most everyone considered them unacceptable as a general replacement for pitons. Clearly they weren't as sound, and anyone making a hard sell for their use in the United States was thought to be a daredevil.

Things changed suddenly. In the early 1970s John Stannard wrote a seminal article illustrating how pitons were rapidly demolishing the rock, followed closely by Doug Robinson's "The Whole Natural Art of Protection," which appeared in Chouinard Equipment's 1972 catalog. Royal Robbins also suggested nuts as the only alternative if the crags were to survive aesthetically. By this time, Chouinard Equipment (now Black Diamond) was mass-producing chockstones, and almost overnight "clean climbing" became the rage. First "clean" ascents of popular big walls became fashionable. Climbers waxed poetic about "artful nutting" and "fair-means" climbing. By 1973 walking up to a free-climbing crag with hammer and pegs was akin to showing up at an Earth First! festival in a bearskin coat.

It is a wonderful thing that the climbing community was quickly won over to clean climbing. The sport was booming and every classic climb was destined to become a ghastly string of piton scars unless nuts replaced pitons as the common means of protection. Within a couple of seasons, clean climbing had reduced a climber's impact on the rock to chalk and boot marks. The benefits were clear, and the change was long overdue.

Unfortunately the nuts available at the time still had serious limitations. Chouinard Equipment's Stoppers and Hexentrics (Hexentrics appeared in '71, Stoppers in '72) were pretty much the whole shooting match, though one could flesh out a rack with oddball European imports that did little more than take up room on the sling.

Recall that in the '70s, American climbing standards came principally from Yosemite, where cracks are generally smooth and uniform. The Stoppers worked well in cracks that were ultra-thin up to an inch in width, but the first hexes (a name later adopted by other manufacturers and now used as a generic term) needed a virtual bottleneck for a fail-safe placement. On long, pumping Yosemite cracks, such constrictions often are few and

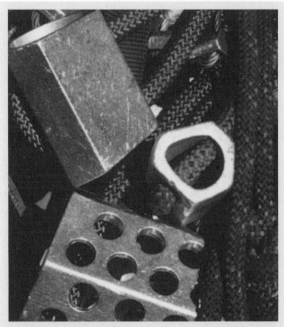

Hexes from the early 1970s. PHOTO BY CRAIG LUEBBEN.

Pin scars on *Serenity Crack,* Yosemite. PHOTO BY BOB
GAINES.

far between, if present at all. From about 1971 to 1973, old testpieces became feared again—not so much for technical difficulties, but because of the lack of protection provided by available nuts. There were a handful of routes where you simply couldn't fall, though more than one climber did, and the scenes were not pretty. Clearly the limitations of these first nuts, coupled with climbing's rising standards, made clean climbing on hard routes a bold prospect during that first phase of the hammerless era.

Then in late 1973, Chouinard changed the symmetry of the hexentric, eliminating the radical taper. The resultant "polycentric" was a nut one could place in four different attitudes (including endwise), and each placement was far more effective than what could be achieved with the old design. These new hexes hinted at the camming to come and brought a degree of security back to the sport.

Subtle changes also were appearing in other chocks. Wire cable replaced rope and sling for the smaller-sized nuts. Manufacturers entered the market with specialized gear—brass nuts, steel nuts, even plastic nuts were available for a short time. New-fangled homemade gear also began appearing, and the race was on for more diverse designs.

The pivotal breakthrough came in 1978, when Friends first became available commercially. The popular story is that Friends evolved from a simple camming device invented by Mike and Greg Lowe in 1967. Ray Jardine, a climber with a background in aerospace engineering, spent much of the '70s refining the concept (the Lowes had the right concept but never produced a workable design), and the first spring-loaded camming device (SLCD) was the result. The era of super-specialized protection had finally arrived, and a protection revolution followed. In the ensuing ten years, SLCDs—more commonly called camming devices, or cams—became available from many manufacturers in various forms and sizes. Also component "sliding nuts" appeared that literally expanded in breadth when weighted in the direction of pull (explained in detail later). Sliding nuts never truly caught on, possibly because they were often difficult to remove.

As other companies sprang up and European companies airmailed ingenious, sometimes kooky contraptions into the American market, passive nuts were steadily improved and customized for specific applications. Sling materials likewise evolved, as did carabiner design and rope technology. Present-day novelties include the DMM revolver carabiner, with a built-in pulley, and the removable bolts now available from Climb Tech, to mention only a few. Yet since the SLCD first arrived on the scene in 1978, there hasn't been any comparable breakthrough in protection technology. Refinements continue with every aspect of climbing tackle. Classic designs are regularly tweaked and buffed and reworked to effective ends. Cams themselves have undergone significant change, with some designs now offering greatly increased range of placement. But the Next Great Thing has yet to appear.

All told, the current state of rock-climbing equipment makes memories of barrel-chested bruisers in lug-sole boots slugging home pitons almost quaint. To catalog all the viable equipment manufacturers would involve adding fifty pages to this book. Simply understand there is fierce competition for your dollar, and to get it, companies are sparing nothing in both technology and research and development. The result is gear superior to most any other adventure sport.

Charlie Henrikson on *Born Under a Bad Sign,* Paradise Forks, Arizona. PHOTO BY STEWART M. GREEN.

PART ONE

SIMPLE ANCHORS

A simple anchor is a one-point anchor—a single nut, spring-loaded camming device (SLCD), sling, fixed piton, etc.—as opposed to combining single-point anchors into the solid matrix of a belay anchor. Because the foundation of all anchor matrixes rests with the simple *primary placements*, the importance of obtaining bombproof simple anchors cannot be overstated.

Appropriate gear, suitable cracks and adequate rock quality are necessary to obtain a solid anchor. Without all three, we're hosed. You might think the absence of good cracks would be the most dire, yet I recall a story from my friend and partner Richard Harrison that illustrates what can happen when the gear is lacking.

Richard and the late, great Nick Escrow were high on El Capitan when, moored at a hanging belay, Nick handed Richard a 1-inch nylon runner containing most all of their rack. To their horror, the knot on the sling came untied, and the entire rack dropped into the void. That left them with about eight nuts and assorted pegs filched from the bottom of the haul bag, and the very anchor from which they dangled. They also were able to clean a couple nearby fixed pins, but the last pitches were extremely touch-and-go as they leapfrogged along, sometimes able to climb but 50 feet before having to stop and belay in a weird and perilous spot, sometimes "anchored" and hauling from a single wired nut. Dreadful. By contrast, on Himalayan alpine routes, a team can have exactly the right gear and ample cracks, but owing to poor quality rock, security is but a dream.

To the layman glancing through the following chapters on the various protection devices, the whole lot may seem bewildering and complex. Yet the basic use of protection usually is straightforward and self-evident. Simply put, you select a section of crack, and place in that crack a protection device of corresponding size. The process is not terribly unlike working those wooden puzzles when we were kids and we stuck the big star into the big star-shaped hole. Since the size of the crack dictates what gear can be used, you instantly can eliminate all gear outside a specific size range. If you're looking at a half-inch crack, you have only to consider options that can possibly fit that crack. Much more on this later.

In the absence of a crack, the rock might offer a suitable protruding or tunneling feature, or a luxuriant tree or bush. In these cases, an anchor may be secured by slinging the natural feature. Of course, an ever-increasing number of face routes have been equipped with bolts, and obtaining anchors on these fixed routes requires only clipping into the bolt hanger, negating the need to place any gear at all. But when the anchor involves hand-placing gear in a crack or rigging slings about natural features, the main goal is to obtain the strongest anchor possible from the given crack or feature.

"Good-enough" anchors require:

1. Suitable cracks
2. Adequate rock quality
3. Appropriate gear
4. Sound primary placements
5. Modern rigging techniques
6. Efficient construction and removal
7. Simple form and function
8. Strength and security throughout the system

CHAPTER ONE

Natural Anchors

Natural anchors consist of anything that the environment provides—trees, blocks, horns of rock, etc. Many times a natural anchor is stronger than anything you could arrange with store-bought gear. Like any other anchor, there are numerous considerations that affect the strength of a natural anchor.

Of the many advantages of using sound natural anchors, three stand out. First, they are typically easy and fast to arrange. You might simply loop or girth a tree or a block (or whatever) with runners. Second, a slung natural anchor is often bombproof no matter the loading direction (multidirectional). Third, natural anchors are usually the least environmentally disruptive means of protection.

> **Natural Anchors are:**
>
> 1. **Anything the environment provides—trees, blocks, horns of rock, etc.**
> 2. **Often more secure than gear-built anchors**
> 3. **Typically easy and fast to arrange**
> 4. **Multidirectional (can be loaded from any direction)**
> 5. **By and large environmentally friendly**

TREES

Anchoring to a 50-foot oak that casts a shadow like a thundercloud is pretty straightforward work. Judgment enters the game once the trees become smaller and are located on top of the cliff, on ledges and on shelves. I've seen some analyses of which trees are best suited for use as anchors; some of these go so far as to study the individual grain of the tree. But most of this—and everything else for that matter—basically boils down to common sense. Still there are several considerations worth noting.

Some climbers think anything with bark on it is bomber, and the infamous Tobin Sorrenson was one of them. It was at Granite Mountain—not the gem in Prescott,

Sharon Sadlier belays Heidi Benton on *Pete & Bob's,* Garden of the Gods, Colorado. PHOTO BY STEWART M. GREEN.

Arizona, but a scrappy little cliff outside Amboy, California, that has for years been closed to climbing. (An old rummy with a 12-gauge full of rock salt stands guard, in case you're wondering.) Tobin was leading up one of those greasy, teetering slabs that look like you could make good time up it in flip flops, when in fact your only hope is to keep your $150 boots bicycling like Wile E. Coyote. When I clawed up to Tobin's belay and saw the anchor, I lost my mind.

"What the hell is that, Tobin?!"

"It's a tree. . . ."

I'd shot pool with a bigger "tree" than this one.

"That's not a tree, it's a twig. A dead twig." And it was sticking out of a clump of orange moss on an angled, shaly little foothold stance. I reached over and yanked the sad thing out with about ten pounds of heft.

"Jesus! You trying to kill us or something?!" Tobin cried.

The point is that what the tree is rooted in is probably more crucial than the breadth of the tree itself. Good-sized trees have pulled out; the big one atop the first pitch of a route called *Catchy,* at the Cookie Cliff in Yosemite, being a case in point. While there is likely no single and reliable way for a climber to know or test how well a tree is rooted, we're left to do a thorough inspection, including shaking the tree to check for movement. While some books have suggested various forestry strategies to establish the holding power of trees, no two trees are the same. I've personally hooked a tractor to a tree no thicker than my arm and only managed to break a chain in trying to yard out the implacable pine. I've also seen trees big around as a pickle barrel come totally uprooted after a thunder shower. Nevertheless we need a few provisional guidelines to help guide our choices.

First, you want a live tree, preferably 6 inches or more in diameter, not one that's been chopped or burned or is rotten. Any tree rooted in shallow soil, gravel, scree, moss or soot, or that's burgeoning from a slim crack, should be considered suspect. If you've no other choice for an anchor—or even if you have—test the tree with a solid shake. Boot it, try to rip it out. If it still feels sound, it probably is. Remember, of course, that a serious leader fall can generate much more impact force than a yank on the tree.

Whenever possible, tie the tree off with slings or a cordelette instead of looping the rope around the trunk. Once you get sap on a rope, it's like a bum rap or memories of love—you just can't shake it. Plus, the pivoting action common when leaning off the anchor can quickly abrade the sheath of a rope. Go with runners or a nylon cordelette.

Unless the tree is truly a whopper, tie it off as low as possible to reduce leverage. Never tie off a tree with a loop of biners. Girth-hitched runners or a cordelette are both popular methods (see photos and illustrations). A cordelette is longer than most slings, negating the need to girth-hitch two slings together to reach around the tree. Although arranging a girth-hitch to connect two slings is simple as rain, a recent rappelling accident in Arizona cost a wonderful young woman

> **When anchoring to a tree . . .**
>
> - **Make sure it is alive.**
> - **Use slings or a cordelette instead of rope to tie it off.**
> - **Tie it off as low as possible to reduce leverage.**

By tying this cordelette off with a figure eight, it essentially becomes redundant, with two loops around the tree. The doubled, power point clip-in helps prevent improper loading of the biner. In all such setups, try to keep the inside angle of the cord/sling less than 90 degrees to avoid load multiplication.

The downside of keeping the inside angle less than 90 degrees is that the longer slings add slack to the system, and unless the tie-in remains under tension (by the belayer leaning off the anchor), the sling(s) can migrate down the tree trunk—not necessarily a bad thing with this atomic bombproof anchor. However as a general practice, after you arrange protection/anchors, you don't want them to move—at all—till removal.

(an instructor with years of experience) her life when she apparently failed to properly girth-hitch two slings together prior to looping the anchor sling around a tree. As with any knot, even one as simple as the girth-hitch, check and double-check your work. And when slinging a tree, tie all knots and get the sling configuration squared away *before* you rig the tree, in order to visually verify all things are "mint." For an extra bomber and redundant setup, and one without the load multiplication of the girth-hitch, rig the tree with two slings and two locking biners. There is no question this is a more secure setup, but most climbers go with the single sling girth-hitch, providing the sling(s) are in good shape and the tree is robust. As always, it's your call.

Trees are generally quite durable—to a point. At Great Falls and Carder Rock, both in the Washington, D.C., area, and at Coopers Rock, outside of Morgantown, West Virginia, trees are used almost exclusively as toprope anchors. Owing to soil compaction and wear and tear on the tree trunks, authorities have considered closing down sections of the cliffside. Climbers have responded by adopting gentler methods of anchoring off trees, such as using scraps of carpet to protect the bark.

Anchoring to a Tree

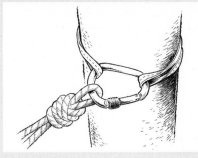

Incorrect. When pulled straight out on, this setup will stress the relatively weak gate of the carabiner.

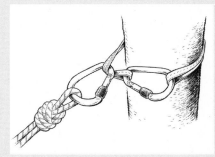

Slightly better, but the sling is overly stressed.

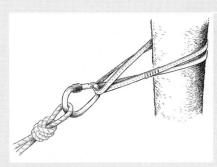

Okay. the sling configuration is strong, but the sling is loose and can easily slip around on the tree. Slide it down around the base for more security.

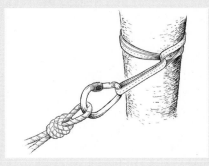

Okay. The girth-hitch keeps the runner from slipping on the tree.

SHRUBS AND BUSHES

Anyone who has tried to clear Grandma's backyard understands the hateful toil of uprooting healthy shrubs and bushes. Hence, they often make good anchors. As a general rule, it is easier and less time-consuming to rig a traditional anchor, providing one is readily available. But if good nuts are problematic to set, and a shrub, bush or sapling is at hand, consider using it.

Again, you want live stuff. Nothing brittle, charred, rotten or loose will do. And make sure the stuff is well-rooted. Most of the time a shrub or bush issues from a central root, and that's what you want to sling. Try to get the sling around that chubby root as near to the base as possible, and cinch it down snug. It is very sketchy to trust a solitary bush or shrub, and since they tend to grow in clumps, tying off to three or four (or more) and equalizing these anchors (to be explained later) is smart rigging. More times than not you'll have to ferret around and push sometimes-thorny limbs aside to get at the main root. Do so. Never settle for less than the best and least-leveraged tie-off you can manage. And always test the bush or shrub with a hearty yank. Unless you test it and test it good, you might be tying off something no more secure than a tumbleweed on a bridal path.

BOULDERS AND BLOCKS

These can provide sound, quick anchors if several things check out, and you follow a few rules of thumb. First, realize that both boulders and blocks are not part of the body of the cliff. They are detached, and the only thing keeping them in place is their size, weight and position. For a boulder or block to be any good at all, it must be both sufficiently big and positioned in a way that it cannot be moved. It should not wiggle or budge at all. Anyone who has trundled boulders off a remote slab knows that a boulder big as a house can be sent on a path of mind-boggling destruction if it's on even the slightest grade. Following the first free ascent of the *Salathe Wall* in 1988, Todd Skinner and Paul Piana nearly died when a huge block they had slung (as an anchor) on the summit of El Capitan migrated several yards down toward the very brink. The duo were lucky to escape with one broken leg between them and a year of flashbacks.

For a leader rigging a belay anchor, caution must be used when tying the climbing rope itself around huge blocks. Watch out for sharp edges and pinches that can severely damage your cord. For toprope setups, most professional guides use static rope when tying off huge boulders and blocks, since it is more abrasion resistant and less

> **Remember . . .**
> - Only their mass and position keep boulders and blocks in place.
> - To serve as secure anchors, boulders and blocks must be sufficiently large and totally immovable.

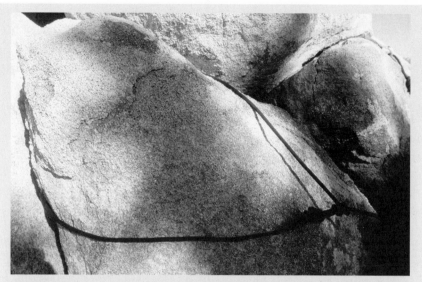

This block is well situated, and is bomber for the direction of pull for which it is rigged. As always, appraising the integrity of a natural rock anchor involves judgment. Carefully examine for cracks in the block. And most importantly, how well is the block attached to the main rock structure? If you decide to use a detached block, how big is it: the size of your car or the size of your boom box? Does it rest on a flat platform or a sloping shelf? As a general rule, many climbers avoid rigging anchors off detached blocks and flakes.

This detached block is gigantic, roughly the size of an outhouse, but is precariously perched on a pedestal slim and angled. The crack between the block and the main wall will readily accept camming devices, but remember this: When you hear about catastrophic anchor failure, the number one cause is bad rock, where someone has committed to a single crack system in dubious rock, or perhaps a tragically loose flake or a detached block. Even the best placements are no better than the rock they are set in.

likely to jam in pinches than webbing. Static rope is also somewhat handier to work with and easier to knot, and it allows you to use a wider range of knots than would work with webbing or sling material. Sometimes the best way to use a block is to encircle the mass of it, tying it off like the ribbon on a birthday gift, instead of running the sling underneath it.

HORNS

We use "horn" here to denote all kinds of protrusions that one might possibly sling for protection. The various kinds are many: flakes, horns, spikes, chickenheads, bosses, bollards, etc.

In this context flakes are simply fragments of rock that are partly or completely detached from the main wall. (Larger flakes might run an entire rope length, or

A quickdraw "thread" tied off directly with a runner. The thread is bomber, because the top of the knob is flush to the wall and the quickdraw cannot slip off. The rock would have to break for this anchor to fail. By hitching a runner directly through the quickdraw, you eliminate a link in the system—a biner. If this setup ever sustained a leader fall, however, the hitch on the runner would get cinched so tightly around the quickdraw you'd likely need a vice and a pair of needlenose pliers to work it loose. Ultimately the strength of this system hinges on the strength of the rock itself. Be careful about threads in desert rock. Entire knobs can pop under the slightest load. PHOTO BY KEVIN POWELL.

WHATEVER THE ROCK FEATURE . . .

- Look out for sharp edges.
- Test the security of the feature by thumping it with the heel of your hand. Anything that wiggles or sounds hollow is suspect.
- Look for surrounding cracks.
- Tie off as close to the main wall as possible, to reduce leverage.
- Tie off with runners, slip-knotting if the form is rounded.

The climbers who made the decision to rap from this flake were lucky they lived to drive home. The structure is completely detached and precariously perched. Structural integrity is paramount when using natural rock anchors, and this one lacks it altogether. This is like building your house on quicksand. Remember: Slings around an "anchor" do not vouchsafe their security.

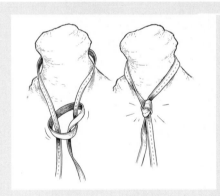

Slinging a horn with a slipknot tied into a runner.

longer.) Hence, it is the position of the flake that is our first concern. If the flake is pasted on a bald wall like a flapjack on a garage door, it's notably suspect. For a flake to be of any value as protection, it must be lodged in a manner that downward pull will only increase its security. Take the standard steps. Eyeball it. Is the quality of the rock okay? No matter how well the flake is lodged or jammed, if the rock is chossy, it may snap in half or crumble once loaded. Thump it carefully, then harder if it's secure. Check for sharp edges. If you decide to sling it, understand that even the best-looking flakes often are unpredictable.

Blocks present the same problems as flakes, with added danger since they are bigger. If you should topple one off, you've essentially sent mortar fire down the crag and possibly onto your belayer. And if you're tied into said block, you're probably going for the ride and the dreaded Dirt Nap. Position is crucial. Look for a block that is keyed into place by the surrounding rock—lodged in a bottleneck is best. Most loose blocks eventually slough off after a winter freeze, but for many years they can remain precariously perched, seemingly held by frozen cobwebs, ready to plummet down the cliff under tread of a piss ant.

Climbers at Joshua Tree toproping off an anchor set behind a loose block. It's no mystery where that block is going to tumble if it comes loose, and it's no mystery what the fate will be of anybody in its path. Although the block is conveniently situated for toproping this route, it is important never to let convenience cloud your better judgment—either find a better anchor or find a different route.

Spikes are pointed flakes or blocks that are usually, but not always, part of the main wall. On well-traveled routes, most of the loose rock has already been stripped away by previous parties, but don't bank on it. The first time I climbed El Cap, Ron Fawcett and I were traversing the Grey Bands on the *Nose,* a sketchy, nondescript section at mid-height where the rock is grainy gray diorite. I was belaying from slings, and as Ron came up, I noted a thick, 300-pound spike just above. It looked funky. I didn't know the numbers but figured the *Nose* had been climbed at least twenty times by then, so all the loose stuff must have been long gone. Not so. When Ron grabbed that spike, it pivoted straight down, and I still don't know why he and the spike didn't land in my lap. Who knows what kept it in place before we came along. The adage is: Never trust anything outright. Always assume it's poor, test it with caution, and only use it when you're convinced it's good. Guides at many trad areas report that many accidents are the result of beginners aggressively grabbing loose rock features without first cautiously testing them. Assume such features are poor, and avoid becoming a statistic.

A boss is a rounded spike or knob; a chickenhead is a knob that often resembles a protruding mushroom; and a bollard is a hummock of rock. The bigger they are, the more probable it is that they are sound—but not always. Depending on the shape of the knob, the hardest part might be figuring out how to tie it off. The more rounded, the less secure. The girth-hitch is usually helpful here.

A chickenhead is as shady as a felon on bail. Approach it with wariness. They usually consist of a mineral or rock type that is more resistant to weathering than the underlying stone. Carefully

This marginal sling is slightly improved by setting a taper on the right to keep the sling in place. However, things look borderline on the left side. When a sling is simply draped over an edge like this, as opposed to being cinched tight with a girth or clove hitch, you want much more substantial purchase. Don't always expect to get it, however. Using the taper to shore up this placement has turned an unacceptable anchor into one that just might hold. But you wouldn't want to count on it. You're better off using the taper as an anchor, equalizing it with the sling. By loading it, you'd improve its ability to hold a sideways tug from the sling. PHOTO BY KEVIN POWELL.

inspect the base of all chickenheads because many are shot through with thin cracks. Thump them gently, then harder. I've had more than a few chickenheads come off in my hands, and several have popped the moment I stepped on them.

Recreational climbers rarely venture onto new or infrequently traveled routes, where the above considerations are particularly germane. As mentioned, most popular routes have long since had most of the loose rock booted away. But never count on it. It took almost forty years for a well-known rotten log to finally fall off the classic *Royal Arches* in Yosemite, and when that monster finally cut loose, it

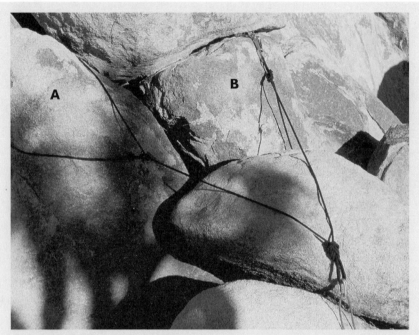

This TR rig consists of A) a natural rock bollard, and B) two camming devices in a horizontal crack. The anchor system is pre-equalized, featuring a static extension rope tied with a double-loop figure eight at the power point. The rope is attached with two oval carabiners, gates opposed and reversed.

Arranging a clean and simple anchor is sometimes tricky among such jumbled terrain. Here the climber decided where she wanted the power point and worked backward from there. The whole rig hangs nicely over the edge, and the use of the static rope is good for added abrasion resistance. The rock structure at A is beefy and well attached to the main rock structure. The two cams at B are solid placements, but if you scrutinize the structure, they are actually underneath a massive, detached block. The use of two oval carabiners opposed and reversed is adequate, but many climbing schools and outdoor programs use three oval carabiners, gates opposed and reversed, as their standard operating procedure.

must have been a sight. Ultimately common sense and a suspicious sense of judgment are your best weapons when dealing with all natural features.

THREADING TUNNELS

When the rock weathers or cracks to form a hole in the main wall, climbers often can exploit the feature by threading a sling through the cavity. Common sense and sticking to the advice already laid down is key here. Is the feature strong? Thump it. Are there sharp edges? Is it cracked? And how big is it? Occasionally something as small as a suitcase handle can provide adequate protection. Anything less should be used cautiously, no matter how stout it appears.

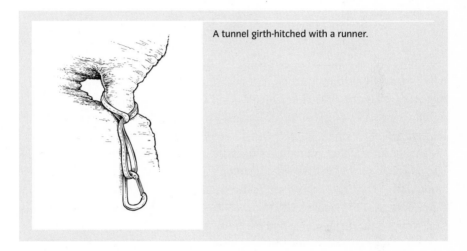

A tunnel girth-hitched with a runner.

CHOCKSTONES

Any rock lodged inside a crack is a chockstone. You appraise the security of the chockstone just as you would that of a nut—does the stone's symmetry correspond to that of the slot? Is the stone set in a bottleneck or a constriction? Will downward loading decrease or increase its purchase? After considering these points, apply the same rules concerning horns, blocks, flakes, etc. Are there sharp edges? What is the quality of the rock? If all things look good, but the positioning is suspect, wiggle the stone around and secure a better seating if need be, *but be careful not to dislodge it*. This is a very real concern with bigger chockstones, and if the thing blows, it's *bombs away!*

Pay close attention to how you sling the chockstone. Often even the slightest tension can cause the chockstone to wobble or rotate inside the crack, and the sling can creep between the stone and the wall and get stuck—or sometimes even

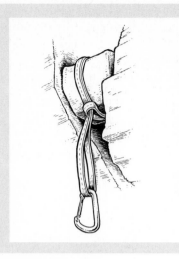

A girth-hitched chockstone. Make sure the hitch is tight around the chockstone and pulled snug against itself so it won't slip if stressed.

pass between the stone and the wall. Chockstones are infrequently used because they rarely meet the above requirements, and can be problematic even if they do. Getting them well slung is often the hardest part. Again the girth-hitch is usually the first option.

Though infrequent, some chockstones are clearly so bombproof that there's no budging them nohow. In these rare situations some guides girth-hitch the chockstone with a sling, jamming the sling's overhand knot between the main wall and the chockstone. The idea is to try to distribute any loading between the knot in the sling (which is acting like a nut) and the chockstone around which the sling is hitched. Though I've never see this technique used in the field, such is the improvisation common to all facets of anchor building.

CHAPTER TWO

Passive Chocks

Much as I'd like to shorthand the purely verbal discussions, the fact is you need to study more than the photos and captions to fully grasp the material. It's not enough to see a photo of an anchor and know how to construct a similar setup. You also have to know *what* you're looking at, in both simple and theoretical terms, and you have to know *why* you do things this way or that. Much strategy goes into placing and constructing anchors, and the nuances cannot be adequately spelled out with the anchors that are already built, as they are in the photos. With this text you learn the theory; in the photos you see that theory applied. Yet it's not enough to discuss or even to see how to make placements; you also must *learn* how to place pro (protection). Trial and error is not the recommended strategy. Developing good hardware-placing skills is a craft requiring diligent practice, and the best way to start is to get a grasp of the material from a book like this, practice placing pro low to the ground (preferably with your feet *on* the ground), and then take an anchor-building seminar (very common these days) from a qualified guide. Such a multipronged approach increases the odds that the material will thoroughly be understood, and that it will stick. For now, bear with these windy breakdowns and see the subject all the way through.

The family of climbing chocks can be split into two categories—passive chocks (or nuts), which emphasize simplicity by having no moving parts, and active chocks (spring-loaded camming devices or SLCDs), which achieve a high degree of utility through their geometry and moving parts. Passive nuts can be further divided into two categories: tapers, and all the rest. Passive nuts wedge into constrictions inside cracks, with the notable exception of Tricams, a sometimes fussy piece of specialty gear—loved by a few, never used by all the rest—that can wedge in a constriction or cam in a parallel-sided crack. The greatest asset of passive nuts is

Tom Callahan on *Separate Reality,* Yosemite, California. PHOTO BY BOB GAINES.

their simplicity. They have no moving parts and are light, compact, reliable and easy to evaluate when placed.

As a primary anchor, many climbers go with the low-tech, passive nuts—when they have a choice. They require less judgment and are easier to appraise with a novice eye. For instance, if the crack narrows like a bottleneck, place a taper in the bottleneck instead of wiggling an SLCD into a parallel section of the crack. Unless the wire fails (almost unheard of in tapers of medium size or greater), or the rock shears away (very unlikely in good rock), there is virtually no way for the placement of a taper in a bottleneck to fail when set for the direction of pull. Again a low-tech approach is almost always easier, more efficient and more secure. Like they say, you don't row a boat with satin gloves.

TAPERS

Tapers are basically six-sided aluminum wedges. Smaller tapers also come in brass and steel, as we'll soon discuss. Present-day tapers of every size are slung with a swaged cable; in years past some tapers were engineered to be slung with cord. Note that one of the recent refinements in tapers is the elimination of overkill in the size of the wire. Instead of attaching a wire the size of a ship's cable, most manufacturers now are going with a thinner, lighter, less-expensive cable. The facts have dictated such a move—after all, given the properties of modern ropes, a normal-sized climber taking the longest possible fall cannot generate an impact force exceeding 2,420 pounds, so why freight the nut with a cable good to 7,000 pounds? Wild Country has noted that for years their tapers (excepting small sizes 1 to 4) featured cable good to "only" 2,220 pounds, yet *not one cable has ever failed in use.*

The first tapers were much wider than they were thick. Now virtually all tapers are of a much boxier design, particularly useful for endwise placements. There are three basic variations on the original straight taper: the curved taper, the offset taper and the micro brass or steel taper. In addition designers have altered the sides of these various tapers. Some tapers feature gouged-out teardrop cutaways, or scoops. Some have been filed or beveled this way or that, like the Metolius Curve Nut, which is tapered side to side as well as top to bottom. Some look like junior high industrial-art projects and are no good at all. The variations are many, but all are meant to be slotted in a crack whose contours approach the symmetry of the nut, with the cable or sling pointing in the anticipated direction of pull. Ironically, most manufacturers have discontinued making the straight taper in anything but the smallest sizes, having found that the curved model is far more stable when placed.

SEVERAL RULES FOR SETTING SAFE CHOCKS— PASSIVE OR ACTIVE:

- The primary rule is that no rock-climbing anchor is 100 percent reliable. Appropriate backups are essential for secure climbing.

- Before setting a chock, look around to find a strong, quick placement, considering all possible directions of loading. Always go for the easiest, most obvious placement, and use a passive nut if possible. Pick a nut that you can place in an easy, straightforward manner, as opposed to making a "creative" placement with a different-sized nut.

- Try and slot nuts in constrictions where, in order to ever pull through, the nut would be reduced to something as thin as beer can aluminum.

- Always visually inspect the placement. If the situation requires, set the piece with a tug.

- Any climbing protection is only as strong as the rock it contacts. Manufacturers report that nuts pull out under frighteningly small loads during testing in poor quality rock. Chocks create a large outward force when holding a fall. Avoid setting anchors behind a shaky flake or block rather than risk pulling it down if you peel off—it's always best to fall alone!

- Try to place the gear in its primary position. Most all passive nuts can be positioned in several ways. Familiarize yourself with the primary, or preferred position, and try to go with that whenever possible. For instance, a taper can be placed endwise, but usually it is not as reliable as one placed the primary way.

- Be especially careful not to dislodge the piece with your body, rack, or rope after you have placed it.

- If you haven't used a certain type of chock before, practice placing it on the ground (extensively) before thumbing it into a seam and casting off for a barndoor lieback.

- No climbing gear lasts forever. Inspect your gear frequently. Retire hardware if you observe cracks or other defects in the metal, or if the cable becomes kinked.

Tapers often are the easiest nuts to place because their design is the most basic. The crack must pinch off in the direction of loading—usually down—to accommodate the taper. Simply try to place the taper that best corresponds to the geometry of the crack where it pinches (the so-called "bottleneck"). Ideally you want a match fit, in which the contours of the crack are precisely those of the taper. Imagine a pea in a pod. Best of all is when the crack pinches somewhat in the outward direction as well. Here the contour of the rock will resist a slight outward tug that could be created by a falling leader, or a belayer shifting about to rubberneck the leader. The ideal placement may be as elusive as the blue moon or the perfect spouse, but good placements are generally plentiful. Dealing with anything but the most deceptive placements is basically a matter of common sense—no need for a bag of tricks.

The more surface area you contact between the rock and the nut, the better. Sometimes, you will have to slot a nut deep in a strangely formed, flaring crack; but if you have a choice, place the nut where you can see exactly what it is set on. With straight tapers you go after the bottleneck placements, or placements where the nut fits like it was milled just for that slot—the proverbial "match-fit." If neither of these placements is possible, try to firmly slot the nut in a constriction where the taper is lodged at about mid-range, or halfway up the faces. If the taper sets too low, say right above the cable, the nut is too big; if it is merely caught on the top 20 percent of the face sides, the nut is too small. Once again go with the taper that best corresponds with the contour of the crack, and try to get as much surface area as possible on the rock. Few rock climbers will ever tell you that size does not matter. And with tapers, always go with the bigger one whenever possible. The cable is probably stronger, and the larger nut will afford more surface area contact and more security. But the principal concern is the placement—be sure the taper fits the crack.

In shallow or flaring cracks, even pros have to tinker around to find the best placement, and this is where endwise placements are most often used. An endwise placement offers less surface area contact with the rock, but go with it if the fit is superior. You might have to, because some cracks are too shallow to accept a normal placement. Again, when the placement is marginal, look for that section of

Both sides of this Stopper have great surface contact, and the constriction of the crack corresponds with the shape of the taper.

Like a man in the wrong-sized trousers, this Black Diamond Stopper does not fit the slot. A desirable placement would involve a larger Stopper normally placed (rather than endwise), with the main faces of the chock flush with the walls of the crack. This nut has all the earmarks of sketchy pro: poor surface contact, susceptibility to an outward force plucking it from the crack and instability from sitting on the flat base of the nut. On a scale of 1 to 10 (10 being bomber), this Stopper is about a 2.

This Metolius Curve Nut has great flushness on the right wall of the crack, but the left side has negligible surface contact on gritty, grainy rock. Dicey! Because endwise placements are generally less stable, always strive to get a flush fit with as much surface contact as possible.

According to Metolius, the design of Curve Nuts, while not technically "offset," gives them added stability in flares. If you should wiggle this nut around a bit, you'd likely find an ideal placement—that's how it usually works. Few cracks are perfectly parallel sided, and slight repositioning can change a marginal placement to something much better—or worse.

crack where the constriction best corresponds with the geometry of the taper. At times you will have to try various tapers to find one that will fit at all, then have to jockey the nut around to locate the best placement, or any placement. On some climbs the hardest part is placing the gear.

Curved tapers are a bit trickier because they present options that straight tapers never did. A little more complicated, yes; but the fact that for twenty-five years they have replaced straight tapers almost exclusively indicates the curved design offers better stability in most placements. The actual curve is hardly radi-

Because the crack is smaller below the taper, the wire would have to break for this Wild Country Rock to fail. Yet this is not ideal because so little of the right side of the nut is in contact with the rock. Here "ideal" does not necessarily mean the placement will hold a harder fall but rather that it will be relatively easy to remove if fallen on—a real world consideration. When a nut of this shape sits on crystals, as this one does, it can get lodged for good when sustaining a stout fall. Even more importantly, a nut is more likely to wiggle out if it doesn't have good surface contact with the rock. PHOTO BY CRAIG LUEBBEN.

cal—usually just a few degrees—and normal placement usually attains an adequately flush fit on the face sides. You should always try to get this match-fit type of placement, but accept the fact that sometimes you cannot.

A straight taper works much like a fist jam in a constriction, where both sides of the fist are lodged between the walls of the crack. A curved taper sets in the crack like a hand jam, with three points of contact; a downward pull achieves a rocker effect that further locks the nut in place. There are several things to understand about curved taper design. (The following discussion can best be understood if you have a curved taper on hand for reference.)

Like a banana, you can place a curved taper two ways on the tabletop, so it curves one way or the other. You have a "left" and "right" option simply by flipping the taper over. In a V-slot, or uniform constriction, the curved taper is placed the same way as a straight one, and the curved design plays no meaningful role. Most any nut will do in a true bottleneck. If a bottleneck or pronounced constriction is unavailable, search out that section of crack that best corresponds with the taper's curve, and place it left or right as necessary for the best fit.

Very few cracks are perfectly parallel, and even the slightest wave or jag may be sufficient to accommodate the taper's curve. But when the crack is truly even-sided, you have to utilize the camming action of the nut. The crack still has to constrict, if only slightly, and you must go after that place where you can get a good three-point setting—a fix on the top and bottom of the concave side, and a firm lock on the convex side. You may have to try both left and right placements before you achieve the best fit. The security of the nut, however, usually is determined by

This Stopper is flush on the left side, but the right side has only about 50 percent surface contact, plus the crack opens up immediately below the placement. This placement is *not* bomber—maybe good enough to hang off, but if this Stopper was all that was keeping you from hitting the deck, you'd best quickly look for other placements.

how much and how well the convex face is set. If the concave side has a decent, two-point attitude, if much of the convex side is set snugly, and if the rock below the point of contact narrows even slightly, the placement is likely sound. If the convex side is barely catching, or if its point of contact is either high or low, the nut is almost certainly marginal. Often you can simply flip the nut around and get a better placement. If this doesn't work, try another type of nut.

Beware that the crack doesn't open up on the inside, where the chock could pull through and slip out below like so much sand through an hourglass. In horizon-

This Stopper is wedged in a bottleneck. In a straight, downward pull, it simply cannot be pulled through the constriction. But the left side of the chock protrudes slightly from the crack, and the right side is less than 50 percent flush. These types of placements are easily dislodged from the crack with even nominal outward force, as the surface contact is minimal and the crack opens up above the placement. When making such placements, a slight downward jerk will get the nut set well enough to withstand upward and outward forces while not making the placement difficult to clean. If there's any doubt, test it by yanking outward and see what happens.

tal cracks, try to find a spot where the crack opens in the back to accept a taper, but pinches off at the lip to hold it securely. Otherwise, place two tapers in opposition (to be covered later). Tugging on a precarious nut may set it and improve its stability, but over-tugging every piece will drive your partners to hard drink as they curse and dangle from their fingertips, trying to remove your jammed gear. That much said, one of the most common mistakes made by novice leaders is to not properly set their nuts and have them rattle out as they claw above.

The business of placing nuts in horizontal cracks requires special attention and will be dealt with shortly. For now understand that nuts are routinely placed this way, but for various reasons. Horizontal placements, alone and in groups, present special challenges and require all the judgment we can muster. Several recent

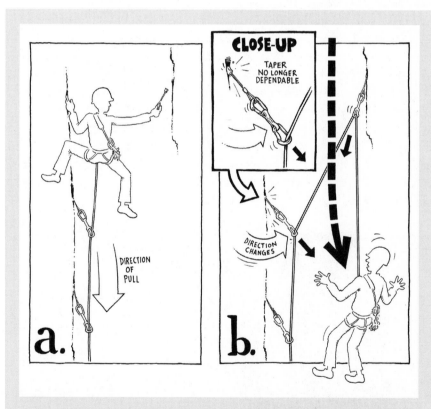

The direction of pull on protection changes with the next placement. In figure A, the falling climber will impact the protection straight down. Figure B shows how a fall on protection placed higher and out of a direct line with pieces below will change the direction of pull. Note that the falling climber will not pull straight down on the top piece because of the placement of the previous nut.

anchor failures, that killed outright all involved, were owing to failed nuts in horizontal cracks.

A last and utterly critical consideration concerns the direction of pull—and this is relevant to all forms of protection, not only tapers. While we are intentionally avoiding discussions that involve the art of leading, the two subjects—placing anchors and leading—naturally overlap. Direction of pull is one of those places.

The question you must bear in mind is: In what direction will your plummeting body, or that of your partner, impact the nut? Obviously gravity dictates that falling objects drop straight down—the proverbial fall line. But chances are, your rope is snaking through a succession of protection below, and that the protection is not in a direct, up-and-down line. Consequently in a fall, each nut is weighted by the rope, which holds the falling climber at the business end. Often a falling leader will first impact a nut with a slight outward pull, then a heavy downward pull (shock loading). Also if the nut beneath the top nut is anywhere but directly below, the direction of pull on the top nut will be downward and somewhat toward that nut (at an oblique angle). It sounds complicated, but it isn't, and the best and only way to determine the direction of pull is to consider the rock as a geometric grid.

If you know where your protection is on the grid, you know that your lower nut is a little to the right or left of your top one, which means a fall will pull the top nut slightly to that side. After a couple of leads you will understand this simple principle. For now it is important that you understand that protection should be placed appropriately for the anticipated direction of pull, or as close to it as possible. The cable or cord coming from the bottom of the nut should point in the direction of pull. More on this later.

Both the ball nut and removable bolt are based upon this concept (opposition). While this configuration ("stacked" Stoppers) *will* work, it is rarely used. In this case these two Stoppers mate together rather well, and both have flush contact with each other and the wall of the crack.

Bearing these points in mind, the business of making the difficult placement simply is a matter of jockeying the taper around in an attempt to best satisfy the aforementioned points. Accomplishing difficult placements is an acquired art, but it doesn't take a wizard to realize a taper hung on a couple of crystals, hanging well out of a rotten crack, is less than ideal.

OPPOSITIONAL NUTS

Imagine yourself climbing up a thin flake, but presently you must traverse off right. You find a nut placement at the top of the flake, but see straightaway that the traverse will put an oblique stress—a sideways pull to the right—on the nut, which is slotted for downward pull. In short, the sideways pull could jerk the nut right out, no matter how many runners or quickdraws you attach to it. And an SLCD won't fit the crack. The normal solution is to place an up-slotted nut and lash it tight to the

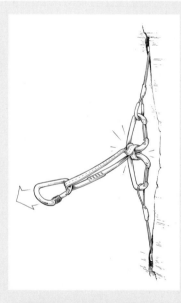

Nuts in opposition, tied together with a clove hitch on a sling, can help solve the direction-of-pull dilemma, especially when an SLCD placement is not available. See the knots chapter for a detailed description of how to tie a clove hitch. This configuration will also work for nuts opposed in a horizontal crack.

Another way to use the clove hitch on oppositional pieces. here the pieces are set farther away, so two clove hitches are used in the sling to tension the pieces against each other. PHOTO BY CRAIG LUEBBEN.

down-slotted, load-bearing nut. The up-slotted nut keeps steady tension on the down-slotted nuts, keeping both securely lodged and providing a multidirectional setup. The hardest part of this operation is almost always attaching the up-slotted "keeper" nut to the other one, while still hanging onto the holds.

Rigging Oppositionals

Opposition can be rigged in vertical, horizontal or even diagonal cracks. Essentially four situations can arise in establishing opposition:

1. You can't find adequate placements at the right distance and the nuts are so close together that they can't hold each other taut. In this case the best you can do is clip both the nuts together with a carabiner. When possible use two carabiners with gates opposed, because of the dangerous triaxial loading on the carabiners caused by this arrangement. Each of the placements must be fairly stable, as no real tension will be placed on the nuts to hold them tightly in place.

2. The ideal situation: The nuts are at the right distance from each other, so they provide natural tautness when cinched with two clove hitches on a $^9/_{16}$-inch or $^5/_8$-inch sewn sling. After rigging this setup, clip into the sewn loop or one of the pieces, whatever best suits the overall anchor setup.

3. The nuts are very secure and don't need to be held taut, so the easiest solution is to simply clip both pieces into the same sling to create a multidirectional anchor. It might be best to arrange the sling to equalize the load with a sliding X, described later in this book.

4. The available nut placements are too far apart, so the pieces must be held together with clove hitches in a section of cordage or a sling. This works, but make sure you analyze the setup well, and crank those clove hitches tight so the nuts hold each other in place.

There are many other possible configurations for opposing nuts—far too many to run down here. The important thing is to understand the few rules of thumb we have laid down: Opposition, tautness and adjusting the length of slings. Exactly how you rig any anchor is ultimately your call, and is case dependent.

Horizontal Opposition

For a nut placed in a horizontal crack to be any good, it must be capable of withstanding some downward pull on the cable or sling, which will result in an outward pull on the nut. In the majority of cases, the loading will be straight out on a nut placed in a horizontal crack. Therefore some part of the crack must taper at the lip, allowing you to wiggle a nut into place, set it with a yank and hope it doesn't shift

Two horizontally opposed nuts (A and B) looped together with a sling (C). Understand this: There is no hard and fast law that we can lay down about just what to do here. Everything is relative to the situation, which differs greatly from anchor to anchor. To ensure security, the first thing you must do is eyeball the nuts and determine from which direction they can withstand the greatest pull. Here the best guide is to consider the wires to be arrows pointing in the direction the given nuts will withstand the greatest impact. The next and all-important task is to rig the system so, in this instance, a downward pull will impact the nuts in the most ideal angle relative to their position (the direction the wires point). This setup is okay to the extent that it accomplishes this.

The downside here is that the upper nut must sustain the bulk of any load. The lower nut is effective only because, by pulling slightly at the upper nut, it redirects the loading onto the upper nut at the best angle. Still, I don't like the looks of this rig. Better opposition between the two nuts is needed. A good solution would be to rig a sliding X on a short sling. Better yet, oppose the nuts against each other with two clove hitches in the sling. Remember, so long as you have an "uphill" nut—as we do here—that nut will absorb most of the force no matter how you rig the tie-off. PHOTO BY CRAIG LEUBBEN.

Here, clove hitches have been tied directly into the two nuts to eliminate undesirable angles of pull on the placements. Not only do the clove hitches allow the sling to maintain an optimum angle of pull on the nuts, but so long as some pressure is placed on the anchor, inward forces between the pieces keep each nut well set. This is one of the best ways to rig two opposing wired nuts in a horizontal crack, a rare scenario but not unheard of on trad climbs.

around and work loose from rope drag. It's often hard to clean these types of placements. When the crack does *not* taper at the lip, one option is to place oppositional nuts. This setup appears much more in climbing books and articles than it does in the field, however, because unless you have two ideal slots closely positioned, it's exceedingly tricky (and typically time-consuming) to rig horizontally opposed nuts that are worth the hassle. The advent of SLCDs has greatly reduced the need to consider horizontal oppositional nuts, but has not eliminated the technique altogether (in quirky circumstances). In over thirty years on the rock I haven't placed horizontally opposed nuts more than a few times, and never in an anchor matrix.

The techniques described above for normal opposition generally work well for horizontal opposition. It's the rigging that is dicey and problematic. Somehow you must rig two opposing nuts—both good for a lateral pull—so they also are good for downward and outward loading. If you have two opposing bottleneck placements, the nuts are probably good, and their placements basic. Here it becomes a matter of rigging the tie-in so the nuts sustain enough tension to keep them well set, usually accomplished by tying the two nuts taut against each other with clove hitches on a sling, and clipping into the sling. If the sling is fairly long—so the two legs of the sling from the nuts to the tie-in carabiner form a shallow angle—then the nuts must be able to withstand a force that pulls them both inward, toward each other and down, or sometimes out, toward the load. If the pieces cannot withstand much of a downward force, using a shorter sling forces the loading more inward, but also increases the magnitude of the force (load multiplication) because the pieces must work more against each other.

Some climbers simply connect the two nuts together with a chain of two or three carabiners. While this may be appropriate in some situations (rarely), it puts dangerous triaxial loading on the tie-in carabiner and forces the loading inward, which may be good for the stability of the pieces, but also may create unnecessarily high forces on them. Furthermore, the carabiner chain does not provide the oft-needed tautness to hold the pieces in the crack when they aren't loaded. If you must use a chain of carabiners, it's best to use two carabiners with gates opposed at the tie-in point. That much said, try to avoid doing so if at all possible, because other, superior rigging methods exist.

Whatever the setup, horizontally opposed nuts are only as good as the weakest nut. Ultimately the only way to be sure is to test them with as violent a tug as is prudent, which, in fact, is but a mere fraction of the forces exerted by a fall. However well we explain things here, placing horizontally opposed nuts takes a lot of practice. You're off to a reasonable start, provided you understand and heed the basics.

OFFSET TAPERS

Offset tapers were developed several decades ago by Hugh Banner of the United Kingdom. These nuts are tapered in two directions, creating a shape that improves security in flared cracks.

The best way to understand this design is to get an offset taper and look at it. You'll find that one edge is thicker than the other—or "offset." Offsets are ideal for flaring cracks that narrow toward the back—like pin scars—where a normal taper would find scant purchase. Be warned, however, that though the offset will work wonderfully when properly set, it is less forgiving in marginal placements, and unless you've got most of the surface area firmly locked, offsets can pop faster than you can yell, "Watch me!"

Originally viewed as a specialty item for use on big aid routes, some free climbers carry a few for those "oddball" placements where nothing else works as well. They were first available only in small sizes, but a dozen or so years ago several manufacturers started offering the offsets in all sizes. The original designers are now

Offset nut.

out of the climbing business; though on a small scale, offset tapers are still made by several outfits. Offsets have their limited place in the protection game, but are likely to remain a specialty item rarely used in normal climbing situations.

MICRO-TAPERS (MICRO-NUTS)

Prudent use of micro-nuts hinges on knowing their limitations. Regardless of what any catalog might tell us, we know at a glance that a wee dollop of brass or steel at the end of a piano wire is, at best, a stopgap device—a last resort when the rock affords us nothing else. The limitations of micro-nuts are matters of strength—the strength of the cable, of the actual nut and of the rock in which the micro is placed.

Amazingly enough, cable strength is the least liability on all but the smallest micros. Cables on the puniest micros are rarely good beyond 500 pounds, if that much. Most manufacturers don't recommend them for free climbing, as even a short fall can snap the cables like so many kite strings. But sizes beyond the smallest feature silver-soldered cables that are good beyond 1,500 pounds and are adequate to survive falls of moderate length. The cables are fragile, however; frays and kinks denote weakening and are sure indicators that the nut should be retired. The cables are particularly prone to fray just beneath the body of the nut, a consequence of the wrenching they take when cleaning them from a climb. Place and remove them gently if you want them to last.

BASIC RULES OF PLACING A GOOD TAPER

- The taper has to be bigger—if only a bit—than the section of crack below where it is lodged.
- Slot the taper that most closely corresponds to the geometry of the crack.
- Whenever possible, set the taper where the crack not only pinches off in the downward direction but also in the outward direction.
- Orient the taper so the cable or sling points in the expected direction of pull/loading.
- Try to get the majority of the nut set against the rock, maximizing the amount of surface contact.
- Avoid endwise placements if possible, as they tend to be less secure.
- If you have a choice, go with the bigger taper, as it is generally more secure, with more surface area contacting the rock.
- Make sure the placement is well seated, with no movement or rattle when weighted by hand.

Looking sketchy there . . . This number 6 Micro Stopper (8 kN or 1,798 lbf) has honorable contact on its left side, but the right side is flush only at the base, making the nut very susceptible to displacement by outward force. Placed like this, the taper cannot be relied on to hold anywhere near its rated strength. A slightly smaller nut might better fit in the bottleneck. If this is all you have, set the nut well with several sharp, downward tugs, bearing in mind you have something on the marginal side, untrustworthy for critical situations—like holding a leader fall.

Whenever you have a choice between two equally secure placements, go with the bigger nut as its component strength is higher. But also understand that the quality of both the rock and the placement are typically what make the nut secure/insecure, not the strength of the cable.

Both nut and rock strength are the limiting factors of micros. Look in any catalog featuring micros and you'll see many disclaimers and explanations. The language can get confusing, so let's look at the situation in simple terms.

Regardless of type or brand, the actual nut head on any line of micros is indeed micro. When you fall—and eventually you will—your weight impacts a very small piece of stainless steel or brass. Depending on how malleable the nut is, and how hard the rock is, several things can happen. With steel micros, even when placed in diamond-hard granite, a moderate fall should not radically deform the nut's shape, because the relative hardness of steel is quite high. However if you place a steel micro in quartz monzonite (Joshua Tree) or sandstone, where rock is prone to shearing away, even the perfectly placed steel micro can rip out, leaving a little groove where it tore through the rock. If the rock is something less than granite or dense limestone, brass micros don't tend to rip out, because the softer brass can deform and bite into the rock. In soft rock, brass micros tend to seat better than steel because of increased friction and bite. In diamond-hard rock, however, softer micros sometimes can't offer enough resistance to the impact force of a stout fall, and they rip out. It's a trade-off, and most climbers own a variety of micros for different situations.

A load-limiting quickdraw, such as the Yates Screamer, can increase the safety margin of micro-nuts or any other dubious gear used for lead protection. The Screamer, and various devices like it, have tear-away stitching that activates at approximately 500 pounds to help absorb and limit the impact force on your protection.

A couple things to remember when placing micros: Anything but a match-fit, where most all of the nut's surface area is flush to the rock, should be considered marginal. The four sides of some micros are nearly symmetrical. For those that are not, endwise placements should be slotted with a prayer.

Know for certain that the smaller micros are used almost exclusively for aid or artificial climbing. Whenever a small micro is used on a free climb, it's always a provisional nut, something to get you to the next good placement—the sooner, the better. There are well-established accounts of micros holding good-sized free-climbing falls, but the reason these accounts live on is because they are so improbable, or more likely, made up. If you're wobbling out there on bleak terrain and a micro is the only nut separating you from eternity, you're not long for this world.

Offset micros always should be considered trick—or specialty—nuts. As mentioned, it is highly advisable to go after the match-fit. Micros have precious little

Because of micros' boxy shape, near parallel-sided cracks often afford the best placements. Careful placement is essential, because the relative differences between a good and bad micro are small indeed. While it is tempting to slot the nut deep in the crack, it's usually better to keep it where you can visually assess the placement. The right edge of this micro appears to make good contact with the rock, but it's difficult to see exactly what is happening on the left edge. It's troublesome to accurately assess many placements without getting your nose right in there and checking it out.

This Black Diamond Micro Stopper has great surface contact on the left side, almost 100 percent flush, and this is what you're looking for. The right side is also nearly flush, plus the nut simply fits the slot. To secure truly bomber placements, scan the crack for the "V-slot" configuration, and place the nut that best fits the slot. Remember to set the placement with several downward tugs, and give it a test by yanking slightly out and up. A poorly seated nut may hold a ton with a straight, downward load, but may be yanked up and out with a minimal force (like rope drag). Review the breaking strengths of the nuts you buy, and take this into consideration when building your anchor. This number 3 Micro Stopper has a breaking strength of 5 kN (1,123 lbf), compared to a number 6 Stopper (10 kN or 2,248 lbf).

surface area to begin with, and you want all of it flush to the rock. This is even more essential with offset micros. If the sides of an offset micro are not lodged fast, it will pivot out when weighted. I learned this on a practice aid route at Suicide Rock, when I took a 30-foot fall and felt like a fool.

Like the larger offset tapers, offset micros are particularly useful in pin scars, where the bottom of the hole is flared and a normal taper would be fortunate to hinge on a couple of crystals. Offsets can lock right into these placements, but you must be able to visually verify the match-fit. If you can, offsets are remarkable.

ALL THE REST

Tapers are designed specifically for small cracks, and are indispensable for cracks up to about ¾-inch wide. The smallest are about ⅛-inch thick, the largest about 1¼-inch thick. Beyond these dimensions, the design becomes prohibitively heavy, and other designs—all the rest—take over.

In larger cracks SLCDs generally offer more utility than passive nuts, but the larger passive chocks, such as hexentrics (which are now manufactured by several companies), or the less-common Tricam, can be useful to complement your cams, particularly on a large rack, or as an economical option for toproping.

Thirty years ago, Chouinard's hexentrics (and later, tube chocks) were the sole option for medium to wide cracks. Now there are several other designs, though camming devices have for the most part replaced all the rest as the nut of choice for medium to wide cracks. Still, new products such as the Metolius Curved Hexes and Wild Country Rockcentrics indicate an enduring appreciation for simple and effective technology. However, the basic design, like that of a mousetrap, hasn't changed much in one hundred years because the original article did the job nicely, and still does.

Hexes

Because the sides of a hex (both regular and curved models) are angled similar to the opposing faces of a taper, you generally can place them using the same rules of thumb that apply to tapers. You want that match-fit, in which as much surface area as possible is flush on the stone. If you look at a hex, you will see it affords two possible placement angles, plus a third if the nut is placed endwise. Chances are, one of these attitudes is going to work if the crack constricts at all. When the crack is especially uniform, the hex works best through the camming action on the convex side. In those rare cracks that are perfectly parallel-sided, you're hexed and have to go with SLCDs.

This is what to look for: great surface contact on both sides, with the curve of the nut form-fitting the slot in the rock. Bomber!

Bomber. Great surface contact. A load on this nut would create a camming effect to further key it into the crack.

A match-fit for this old hex; it's flush with the crack, in a slight constriction, and near the lip for easy removal. Since the nut is not in a bottleneck, however, its place-ment is prone to wiggling out with even nominal rope drag, as are similar placements. Set the nut with a good tug. The holding power is not in question, only getting the hex to stay put. Remember, if the crack were only slightly more parallel, the nut could slip down into the opening below. PHOTO BY KEVIN POWELL.

You couldn't hang your hat on this dud—a common type of endwise placement with beginners. The right side is flush against the wall of the crack, but look at the left side! *Minimal* surface contact. This nut simply does not correspond to the geometry of the crack and would likely fail if loaded. A little higher and deeper in the crack a bomber placement awaits . . .

Good endwise placement—flush contact on both ends, well seated and bomber. Set it well and you're good to go.

Tricams

The beauty of the Tricam is its ability to work in both parallel and constricting cracks, and its uncanny knack for fitting where nothing else can. The Tricam design is meant to create a stable tripod with the two parallel camming rails flat against one side of the crack, and the fulcrum or "stinger" point contacting the opposite side, preferably in a dimple of small feature in the stone. For placement in parallel-sided cracks, Camp USA, who took over manufacture of Tricams from Lowe Alpine, advises: "Cock the Tricam by running the sling down the cam channel. Look for a rugosity of some sort on which to position the fulcrum point. (This is not absolutely necessary, but often makes the placement more secure.) Give a good jerk on the sling to set the nut."

Rock hardness, crack taper and flare will affect the security of a given placement. If the placement is prone to sideways or outward pull, sling the Tricam, or extend it with a quickdraw. Practice is necessary to judiciously place the Tricam with one hand. Many climbers consider the unit a somewhat screwy, often fussy

A well-placed Tricam set in the "taper mode." This piece should remain stable in its placement. If you fall on this one, though, it will be rugged to get out. PHOTO BY KEVIN POWELL.

The crack is a bit too parallel for the Tricam to be used like a taper, and it seems to open up just below the piece, which is kind of spooky. A smaller Tricam set in the "cam-ming mode" would be better, or perhaps this one could be cammed with the point seated in the depression just below the piece. An SLCD might be the best bet here. PHOTO BY KEVIN POWELL.

This Tricam is set in its camming mode and will hold a downward pull; however this piece might fall out if it receives a lot of sideways rope wiggle.

specialty item; those who climb rock heavily featured with horizontal, seamy cracks, or pockets and *huecos,* swear by them (though the second on the rope can find them intractable).

Tricams are particularly useful in areas like the Gunks because when they are buried in a horizontal crack, only a soft sling runs over the lip of the crack, as opposed to a cable. In horizontal cracks, in the absence of a sharp edge (that may denude or cut the sling), many climbers try and place Tricams nose down. This often puts less of a bend in the sling contacting the rock. Tricams are sold in eleven overlapping sizes. The smallest four feature color-coded, anodized heads and lighter-weight Dyneema slings. (For more on Dyneema, see the Webbing section later in the book.)

The smaller Tricams—numbers 0.5 through 2—are the most useful and the most stable. Used as belay anchors, they allow the climbing team to save SLCDs for the lead. At 9.4 ounces, the largest unit is quite a load, and the larger units tend to be less than perfectly stable. Tricam slings cannot be readily replaced, unless you send them to a company such as Yates Gear, which professionally replaces the slings.

The Tricam's ability to literally bore into soft rock and avert disaster is best illustrated by another story from the field. Craig Luebben told me that one of his most terrifying moments came on the second ascent of the beastly *Silmarillion,* in Zion Canyon. "I was groveling up a sandy piece of desert offwidth, ready to pitch off, with only a number 7 Tricam between me and my belayer 70 feet below. Suddenly the Tricam popped out and caught on my boot. Eying the chopper ledges in my landing zone, then the ground some 800 feet below, I squirmed like hell to fetch the Tricam. I had no other gear to fit the crack, and downclimbing was out. After some world-class squirreling, I finally snagged the piece, reset it and fell. I frigged the rest of the lead, afraid to move an inch above the precious but shuddering Tricam." He finished off the route then went back home and invented the Big Bro.

Big Bros

The Big Bro is a spring-loaded tube of 6061 aluminum for use in wide cracks. Its minimum breaking strength is over 3,200 pounds. Six sizes provide an expansion range from 2.7 to 18.4 inches.

Craig Luebben, the inventor, is a throwback—a climber who savors offwidth cracks and chimneys. What started out as a senior honors thesis for his engineering degree has been refined into the most effective—and virtually the only—mode of protection for cracks bigger than 6.5 inches. The Big Bro appears to be simply a spring-loaded tube chock, but it's much more than that. Though it takes some preliminary fiddling and experimenting to get the knack of placing a Big Bro quickly

This Big Bro, made by Trango, is well set in a small parallel section of this flared crack. With the ends of the Big Bro solidly in contact with the rock (like this), and with the collar tightly cinched, this placement will hold any direction of pull. Big Bros now come color coded for easy size identification. PHOTO BY CRAIG LUEBBEN.

and correctly, each unit comes with a pamphlet on use, and a climber can get the hang of it in a matter of minutes.

A set of six Big Bros weighs nearly 3½ pounds, and will set you back almost $500, but they work like magic, and the alternative is nearly always no protection at all. The number 2 Big Bro alone provides nearly the same expansion range as an entire set of the old Chouinard tube chocks, and the number 4 has a greater range than a whole set of traditional cams. For wide cracks, the Big Bro is as revolutionary as the first Friends were for smaller cracks.

AID IT

One of the best ways to understand how good, or bad, your placements are is to grab a big rack of nuts and aid climb a popular 5.10 crack (make sure it's a steep one). If you don't know how to aid climb, go with somebody who does. It is one thing to practice slotting nuts and eyeballing them on the ground. But the real learning begins once you start weighting the same placements. The exercise is self-evident the moment you put your weight on the nut.

REMOVING PASSIVE CHOCKS

To remove passive nuts, first try a gentle approach, wiggling the piece out the way it went in. If a taper is stuck, you might try a slight upward tug. But remember, jerking in any direction other than straight down from the bottom of the nut may kink or even break strands of the cable (resulting in hateful "wild hairs," little filaments of sharp cable that can and will prick your chafed fingers like porcupine quills).

If the piece still won't come out, try loosening it with increasingly harder nudges from a nut tool. Nut tools come in a variety of shapes and styles. All the good ones feature a hook-shaped end that is capable of pushing, pulling and otherwise prodding a stubborn nut loose, plus a hole for tying a keeper cord. A nut tool will more than pay for itself by helping you avoid losing stubborn gear, and it is a standard item on many climbers' racks. If a taper is apparently stuck fast, place the end of a nut tool against the wedge itself, and tap the other end of the tool with a large nut, fist-sized rock, carabiner or other object. If the piece moves but won't come out, it's a matter of fiddling with it until you stumble across the same path and orientation in which it was placed. If the piece still won't come free, better to leave it before you completely trash the cable, so it will be of use to future parties. Someone more crafty, persistent or lucky might be able to clean it from the cliff.

Top: Black Diamond. Bottom: Metolius. Without a nut tool, you'll struggle to clean small, well-set nuts. Nevertheless many climbers rarely use a nut tool. To speed removal of larger nuts, tap with a carabiner, large nut, or fist-sized rock in the opposite direction (usually upwards) for which the nut was set.

Rick Bradshaw on *You're Scaring the Horses,* Diablo Canyon, New Mexico. PHOTO BY STEWART M. GREEN.

CHAPTER THREE

Mechanical Chocks

In contrast to the simple looks and what-you-see-is-what-you-get mechanics of passive chocks, the ingenuity of the high-tech gear described in this chapter would impress Da Vinci. The bottom line, however, is that when properly placed, they work great, especially in places where nothing else can.

SPRING-LOADED CAMMING DEVICES (SLCDs)

The only way to get a clear mental image of an SLCD is to get one and start pulling on the trigger. Though there's a lot of artful engineering packed into every cam, the basic mechanics are simple. Currently SLCDs are made by many companies, each with a slightly different look and slightly different features. But all involve a stem (or two) and cams, and the similarities are far greater than the differences in design. Briefly, most SLCDs are shaped similar to a capital T. The top (horizontal) part of the T features a solid axle on which are arranged either two, three or four opposing, teardrop-shaped lobes. The vertical part of the T is the stem (there are both rigid and flexible-stemmed SLCDs), featuring a triggering device that allows you to adjust the span of the spring-loaded lobes. Each unit has a minimum and maximum degree of latitude, and each is adjustable within those parameters. With a full selection of SLCDs (including Wild Country's Zero Size, the Z1), you have a rack that can be micro-adjusted to perfectly fit most any size crack from about $^{13}/_{64}$ inch to 6½ inches. Again it's best to get several of these units in hand to understand fully how they work. Once you grasp the basic principles, SLCDs are perhaps the easiest, most functional and certainly most adaptive pieces of equipment on your rack.

Historically the advent of the SLCD marked the start of the protection revolution, and in terms of gear, it was rivaled only by the development of "sticky" boots in the technical advancement of the sport. That was more than twenty-five years

Ian Spencer-Green on *Dickie Gets It Done,* Big Creek Canyon, Montana. PHOTO BY STEWART M. GREEN.

ago; perhaps nothing in the near or distant future of protection devices will have the instant and significant impact of SLCDs.

Great secrecy surrounded the arrival of the original Friend, the first commercially viable SLCD (the Lowe brothers sold one briefly, but it performed poorly and quickly disappeared). Friends were developed over a period of several years by Ray Jardine, a climber as odd as he was talented. Ray always had to enlist other climbers to help with his many projects throughout Yosemite, ventures undertaken with all the stealth of a *coup d'etat*. The real secret, however, was not the new route, but the queer tackle on Ray's rack. Partners were sworn to secrecy over Ray's prototypes, and Ray made them do everything but sign a contract in triplicate that they wouldn't filch the concept (as Ray had apparently done from the Lowe brothers years earlier), tool up and start cranking out the newfangled widgets for commercial ends. I remember John Bachar climbing halfway up the *East Face* of Washington Column to try to clean a fixed Friend. He got it, too. The next year we all had them, and Ray sailed for Palau on his 80-foot schooner. Never saw Ray again.

In short, SLCDs work by translating a downward/outward pull to an even larger force against the walls of the crack; this in turn creates friction between the rock and the nut, thereby resisting the pull. (Just get one and look at it, and all will become clear.)

The chief advantage of SLCDs over passive protection devices is the speed and relative ease of placing them in a crack. But just because you can get almost instantaneous placement does not mean the protection is secure. The majority of SLCD placements are sound and straightforward, but for those tricky placements, it is essential you know the limitations of the devices, as well as some general rules of thumb that apply to all camming units.

Three or Four Cams, Flexible or Rigid Stems?

Most SLCDs are four- and three-cam units, though two-cam units are also available (but are used far less). Four-cam units have two sets of opposing lobes, or cams, situated along the axle, whereas three-cam units feature a single middle cam opposing the two outside cams. Four cams provide the best strength and stability, while three cams reduce the unit's profile to allow placement in shallow cracks.

This BD Camalot fits this pocket like a pea in a pod. All four cams have magnificent, flush surface contact, and the range of retraction is about 50 percent. To maximize the holding power of the unit, look for each of the cams to contact the rock at lower to mid expansion range (50 to 90 percent *retracted* for Camalots). All cams are a little different, so be sure to read the manufacturer's guidelines on placement for whatever brand you buy.

green=go

yellow=caution

red=stop

Camming devices should be placed in the tighter aspect of their range. This flexible-stemmed Metolius unit has colored dots (drilled holes) on the rim of the cams; this placement sits on the borderline between the yellow (caution) and green (go) dots. Remember, *tighter* is better (although leave the last 10 to 25 percent of retraction for removal). The ideal placement is often when the bottom tips of the cams are in line with each other.

Any camming device is "flexible" if the stem is not rigid. There are several reasons why flexible camming devices were invented. First and foremost, a rigid stem is a liability in pockets and in horizontal, diagonal or shallow placements. When odd angles or torque is involved, a fall can wrench the unit in strange ways, bending or even breaking (rarely) the rigid stem, or—more commonly—ripping the unit from the rock. In thin placements the stem is sometimes thicker than the crack, making placement impossible. A cable stem gives the unit a thinner profile and greater placement utility.

Also contributing to the development of flexible camming technology is the matter of economics and the trigger design patent on rigid-stemmed devices, originally held (now expired) by Wild Country. Individuals who wanted to make camming devices couldn't afford to tool up like a big company. By using cable (which was inexpensive and readily available in small amounts), they eliminated a machined or cast part and were able to create a trigger design that didn't infringe on Wild Country's patent. Oddly enough, these monetary hardships and patent considerations led to many of the refinements in flexible camming devices, because budding manufacturers were left to solve problems creatively, rather than by throwing dough at them.

It is not entirely fair to contrast rigid-stemmed camming devices with flexible units because the applications are different. Rigid units won't work in ultrathin cracks because the stem is too big. Flexible-stemmed units generally will work fine in wider cracks, though not as well as rigid units. But to claim a flexible unit cannot provide adequate protection in anything but thin cracks is untrue. The issue becomes more involved with flexible units that feature a double stem. Though indeed flexible, they offer more stability than a single-cable stem, but still are less predictable (in terms of loading the cams) than a rigid stem. All told, double-stem units are not designed for shallow, vertical cracks, where the stems of the unit protrude horizontally from the crack. The single flexible stem is much better suited for this and other situations, leading to recent design changes—namely, the Black Diamond Camalot Jr., and the Wild Country Zero, which have both changed to a single flexible stem design. Many climbers have noted over the years that the Metolius double-wire stem design protects the cable triggers from wearing out prematurely, whereas the designs previously used by Black Diamond and Wild Country were far less wear resistant.

In terms of use, differences between rigid- and flexible-stemmed camming devices are obvious. Performance differences are less obvious, and debatable. It was once believed that rigid devices have a strength advantage over flexible-stemmed units. That might have been the case a dozen years ago, but no longer. Different makes have different specs, of course; but all American- or British-made SLCDs employ quality materials and craftsmanship, so the relative strength of rigid stems versus flexible stems often is overstated.

As noted, the primary difference is that rigid-stemmed units cannot be placed where the impact of a fall will stress the stem, other than along its vertical axis—for instance, in a horizontal placement where the stem is set over an edge, and

YOU SHOULD KNOW THIS MUCH ABOUT FLEXIBLE CAMMING DEVICES:

- They are less durable than rigid units. Under the impact of a fall, the cables can sometimes kink and/or become permanently deformed.

- The action of the flexible units is less positive because of the inherent flex. This can make placement and removal more difficult, particularly when a climber is fagged.

- It is impossible for a flexible cable to load the cams as predictably as a rigid stem does—or so it would seem. Wild Country claims to have overcome this problem on their Technical Friends, using stronger springs and incremental increases in cam-head width that resist rotation as a climber moves past the placement. This, they say, combined with the single axle and frame that supports the stem, ensure the cams are always loaded in the best possible plane of rotation.

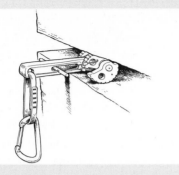

Incorrect use of a rigid-stemmed Friend in a horizontal placement risks shearing the stem.

Not an ideal fit for this rigid-stemmed Friend; a bigger unit should be tried, or this piece should be moved to the right, where the crack is a little thinner. The inner lobe on the left side is nearly maxed out, but the others look better. Flexible-stemmed units were designed for horizontal placements like this. Given that a climber will probably pass over this placement, or will belay below it, the loading direction is straight down, and any load could bend or tweak a solid-stemmed unit like this one. Here the problem has been solved by tying the unit off short with some cord (the "Gunks tie-off"). Understand that even when all things check out, horizontal placements tend to be the most problematic for SLCDs. PHOTO BY KEVIN POWELL.

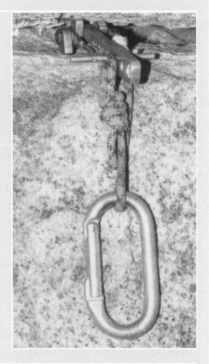

The best option on a horizontal cam placement is to go with a flexible-stemmed unit. It can withstand a downward bend.

where a fall will bend or even break it. Avoid these placements. Wild Country warns against placing its rigid-stemmed Forged Friends in horizontal placements, but offers some suggestions that can make the prospect more acceptable if you have no alternative: First, place the unit as deeply as possible in the crack. Second, if the stem runs over the edge, use a Gunks tie-off, which consists of 5.5mm cord tied through the stem up near the cams.

Finally, Wild Country warns that any Friend, rigid- or flexible-stemmed, placed in a vertical shallow (bottoming) crack where it is impossible to align the stem in the direction of anticipated loading, will have its holding power seriously compromised.

The promotional materials on SLCDs, while useful, can be misleading, especially in terms of strength. The real question is not the absolute strength of the component materials, but how well (secure) the device holds in the crack. Since most tests are conducted in a shop (using a jig), and because the rock affords a virtually unlimited variety of placements, most of the testing can only prove the strength of component parts (the axle, etc.), as opposed to how well the unit will perform in the field. Consequently, shop tests only tell us so much. It should be noted that a properly placed SLCD very rarely breaks. It's almost unheard of that a fall has reduced a device to a glob of bent cams and blown-out springs. Most often the unit has simply ripped out of the rock for any number of reasons. A recent Metolius catalog stated that "rock strength accounts for what is probably the most common mode of failure in the real world. Even in very hard rock types it is not uncommon for the surface layer of rock to pulverize under the force of the cams, forming a loose layer (like ball bearings), which allows the cams to pull out." Thus when you read claims of stronger SLCDs, the propaganda generally refers to the component parts, and not the unit's effectiveness under the stress of a fall out in the field.

Each cam on every SLCD is individually spring-loaded—regardless of the axle configuration, whether it's a three- or four-cam unit, or is equipped with a rigid or flexible stem. The degree of expansion or contraction of one cam is not affected by the position of the other cams. This allows the unit to accommodate size irregularities inside the crack with little loss in stability. The first camming unit, the Friend, was designed to provide quick protection in parallel-sided Yosemite cracks. But there are many climbing areas besides Yosemite, and most cracks are not parallel-sided. When the inside of a crack is even slightly wavy, the individual cams on SLCDs adjust automatically to the irregularities. That is, the cams will be deployed at varying widths. When this happens, as it often does, certain things must be remembered to ensure sound placement.

Though most camming devices feature a constant, or nearly constant angle at which the cams meet the rock throughout their expansion range, the safest and most secure placement is when the cams are retracted as far as possible while still

This Camalot is retracted only about 10 percent. Based on the "constant camming angle" (engineers call it the logarithmic spiral), a camming device will theoretically work at any point in the range. Throughout the cam's rotation, a line drawn from the axle to the cam's point of contact (with the wall of the crack) will remain at the same angle to a line drawn perpendicular from the stem. However the most secure placements will be those in the lower to mid expansion range (50 to 90 percent retracted). Try to shoot for placements where the bottom tips of all four cams come into line. With all camming devices, tighter is better, though if you don't leave at least 10 to 25 percent off the tightest retraction position, you'll likely never get the unit out.

Here a larger camming device is called for. And if this is all you've got—beware. If loaded directly downward, the unit may be strong. But this unit lacks stability and security, as the cams are not adequately supported, and the unit could possibly twist out of the placement and fail.

Also beware of the walking phenomenon. The action of a rope wiggling through a carabiner (or the repeated falling or lowering of someone on a toprope) can force a placement like this to pivot back and forth and "walk" upward. If the crack is wider above the placement, the cams can possibly open even further, rendering the placement worthless. A long sling can help prevent this, but not eliminate the possibility altogether. Avoid situations where the camming device may walk into a wider section of the crack, and look for that sweet, tightly retracted placement, ideally in a pod or a crack with parallel-sided walls.

This Camalot is retracted about 50 percent. Think of 50 percent as a starting point—shoot for 50 percent or tighter. This placement could be improved simply by placing it slightly higher and deeper in the crack. Avoid placing camming devices on the edge of a crack (particularly in soft rock like sandstone), and look for placements in the most parallel-sided spot in the crack, avoiding any flares like the one directly below this placement.

leaving 10 to 25 percent unretracted to facilitate removal. Be careful not to stuff a piece into the tightest placement it can fit, lest you sacrifice a $50 (at least) piece of gear. In an irregular-sided crack, maneuver the unit around so the cams are deployed as uniformly as possible. Remember that even moderate rope drag can cause the unit to walk, or move around in a crack. Because an SLCD will often auto-align to accommodate a new direction of pull, some climbers consider them multi-directional. The problem is that rope drag can also auto-align the unit into an unfavorable position. Bear this in mind. In a wavy crack, even meager movement can radically alter the position of the cams and render the placement poor, or even useless.

While Wild Country recommends its cams be placed between 25 to 75 percent retracted (the middle half of the expansion range), Black Diamond suggests 50 to 90 percent retraction for their Camalots, which reflects the difference between a double-axle (BD is the only one) and single-axle design. Other manufacturers have recommendations specific to their own devices. Read the guidelines that come with the unit.

Some manufacturers alter these cam-deployment recommendations somewhat for really small camming devices, such as Metolius micro TCUs and Power Cams. Metolius says it is critical to place these tiny units near their full retraction and only trust them to hold in hard, solid rock types. The company also notes their units have a slightly smaller cam angle than most manufacturers, so the cams are generating more outward force for a similar load. They believe the increased outward force of the cams, and thus increased holding power, is worth the slight decrease in range. Metolius also touts its cam faces as being the widest on the market, which helps to spread the force on the rock, thus reducing the chance of failure due to rock breakage.

There are several configurations a camming unit can assume that spell danger—or at least trouble. As mentioned, one of the most troublesome positions is when the cams are fully closed inside the crack. That means no matter how hard you pull on the trigger, you can't suck the cams in any tighter, you can't loosen the unit and you probably can't get it out. It's not unheard of for excessive rope drag to put enough tension on a unit that it walks itself into this full-closed position. Much more common is when a hysterical climber shoves too big a unit into too small a crack. Sure, the unit will most likely hold a fall, but removing it probably will entail holding someone on tension so both hands are free to spend a good long time cursing and jerking the unit this way and that. Again, when placing cams, leave some room in the range for removal. Because micro-camming units feature a limited expansion range and must be placed near full retraction or they might pull out, particular care must be taken to avoid getting these units stuck. You have much less room for error because the cams only expand a little, requiring you to make placements with the same precision as with a tricky taper placement.

Offset Cams

Offset cams always should be avoided. This occurs when one cam is near minimum range, and another near maximum. (Don't confuse the concept of unintentionally offset cams with deliberately manufactured offset cams, which are made for flaring cracks—see upcoming section on flaring and tapering.) Beware of this happening in wavy cracks, when the cams must adjust to extravagant differences in crack size. If such a placement is your only option, try a passive chock. Offset cams can also occur in parallel-sided cracks. Remember, if you split the difference, the cams would be at 50 percent—or optimum range—so it's not a problem of size. Instead, the cams have been forced or wrenched into offsetting positions, which renders the placement worthless, or nearly so. When the lobes of any cam approach 80 percent deployment, it only takes minimal movement for the cam to invert. Although modern cams have cam-stops to prevent this, the best policy is to consider placements worthless when the cams are radically offset, inverted or nearly inverted.

This Camalot placement has several problems. While the rock looks sound, the outer cam on the left wall of the crack is too close to the edge. The real problem, however, is the violation of this rule, listed in the Black Diamond literature under BAD PLACEMENTS: "Never place a unit so that the cams are offset, e.g., with two cams extended and two cams retracted. It may not hold a fall."

Strive to keep the loading axis (the axle) near the middle. That is, when the SLCD is placed, it forms a shape, and you want the axle to be pretty much dead center in that shape. If the axle is too far to one side or the other of the cam lobes, the physics are all wrong and the loading is unstable.

Color Coding

Tom Cecil, of Seneca Rocks Mountain Guides, first introduced the idea of color coding cams. He took the larger units, painted them red at each end, yellow toward the middle and green at dead center. This technique works wonderfully—he could know at a glance the orientation of the cams. In the near future I expect to see this method used—in some way, shape or form—by all SLCD manufacturers (as opposed to the far subtler dot patterns). Paint does wear off, so the exact solution is probably a ways off.

Tipsy

Avoid "tipped-out" placements, where the cams are fully, or nearly fully deployed. No camming device is capable of functioning correctly when the cams are at maximum expansion, except the Black Diamond Camalot, which has the requisite strength but virtually no stability in this position and is never recommended to be placed this way. Other units are simply too small for these placements. A fall often will stress the unit just enough to make the cams invert, and the unit will either blow out like a wind-blown umbrella, or the unit will walk to an opening in the crack and become utterly worthless.

As mentioned, the security of a cam is only as good as the position of the cams combined with the relative soundness of the rock. When the unit is placed too deep, the trigger is hard to reach and the unit is that much harder to remove, hence the need to place the unit near the outside of the crack, or as near to that as placement allows. In soft desert sandstone, however, it's best to set the SLCD somewhat inside the crack, so an impact on the piece won't blow out the edge of the crack.

There is a lot of talk about the ability of camming units to swivel toward the direction of pull, once weighted. In many cases this is true, and the cam then becomes a multidirectional anchor. The swiveling action will often align the cams for maximum strength and stability. But the fact is, you should avoid letting your

This old-style rigid-stemmed Friend is too small for the crack, obvious because the second lobe from the front is "tipped out." As mentioned, when the lobes are at or near the limit of their possible breadth, the unit is considered marginal. Even the slightest rope drag can pivot the piece enough for the lobe to invert, like a sprung umbrella, rendering the unit worthless. Often you can jockey the unit around and find a better placement. If not, use a bigger unit. Fact is, you climb long enough and you'll inevitably have to make just such a placement. The crack will be just this size, and the only unit left on your rack will be too small. Place it, trying to find the narrowest place in the crack. It may hold. But understand that you are hoping the unit performs beyond the specs for which it was designed.
PHOTO BY KEVIN POWELL.

Here the rock is solid and the placement looks bomber. But the gate on the biner is contacting the rock and could possibly open when loaded. Remember that when a carabiner is loaded with the gate open, it loses two-thirds of its strength. By looping a sling through the SLCD using the "basket" configuration (see below) this problem is easily remedied.

Solution to above problem.

protection swivel, because a shock load may swivel the unit straight out of the crack, especially if the crack is wavy. *Take special care to anticipate the direction of pull, and to align the unit accordingly when you place it.* Basically—as is the case with all protection that is not beaten into the rock—place the unit with the stem pointing in the anticipated direction of pull, and do whatever is necessary to ensure rope drag won't set the unit to walking inside the crack. Even nominal rope drag can change the unit's position, so most all camming units come with sewn slings. (Those that don't should be connected to the rope with a quickdraw when leading.)

The sewn slings have less bulk than knotted slings, and they can't come acci-

THE BASIC ESSENTIALS OF PLACING SLCDS

- Always align the unit with the stem pointing in the anticipated direction of pull.

- To keep the unit from "walking" because of rope drag during a lead, clip a quick-draw into the sewn sling of the unit.

- Try to place the unit near the outside edge of the crack, where you can eyeball the cam lobes to determine their position. This also makes it easier to reach the trigger to clean the device.

- Strive for the ideal placement, with the cams deployed/retracted in the most uniformly parallel section of the crack, so the cams cannot open if the unit walks a bit. Metolius puts color-coded dots on the cams to help with lobe positioning, but with others you'll have to eyeball it. Read and follow the manufacturer's recommendations for cam deployment.

- Use a larger device over a smaller one, but, unless you are absolutely desperate, never force too big a unit into too small a hole. Once the cams are rolled to minimum width, removal, if possible, is grievous.

- Never trust a placement where the cams are nearly "tipped" (the cam lobes almost fully deployed). In such a position there is little room for further expansion, and stability is poor.

- Never place a rigid-stemmed unit so the stem is over a lip. A fall can either bend or break the unit. If no other placement is available, use a Gunks tie-off (see text and photo).

- Take some time to experiment with marginal placements on the ground. Clip a sling into the SLCD and apply body weight to discover just how far you can trust it. But remember—body weight testing is far milder than a lead fall!

dentally untied. Inspect the slings regularly to make sure they are in good shape. A few companies, such as Yates Equipment, specialize in replacing the webbing on SLCDs. If you use your own supertape, employ a water knot, but keep your eyes on the tails because they will creep toward the knot. High-tensile cord of the 5.5mm variety can also be used to sling an SLCD. For the high-tensile cord the manufacturer recommends a triple fisherman's knot. Rigid Friends are intended to be slung in the large hole in the stem on the opposite end from the cams. An exception would be the aforementioned Gunks tie-off, where the cord is run through the hole nearest the cams to reduce the leverage on the stem when making placements in shallow, horizontal cracks.

Flaring and Tapering

Camming devices work in flaring cracks if the rock is sound and the flare is not so radical that the cam lobes cannot attain adequate bite. When a crack nears the critical flare angle, a fall will load the unit in an unstable manner. If the rock is poor as

This Camalot is placed in the middle of its expansion range, but the crack widens appreciably just above the unit. A little rope wiggle could walk the piece up into the opening, rendering it useless. A taper or hex would fit better in a crack that constricts like this, whereas this camming unit would be better placed in a more parallel section.

well, the placement can sheer out; even in dense granite, the unit can fail if the flare is too great.

With outward flaring cracks—where the lip of the crack is wider than the depths—you should jockey the unit around to find that spot where the difference in cam expansion is the least. If the rear cams are rolled tight, and the outside cams nearly tipped, you're looking at some pretty sketchy pro. Though two cams actually can hold a fall, the unit tends to pivot when the other cams fail, and this pivoting can dislodge the unit altogether.

For tapering cracks—where the crack is wider below the placement—a couple of hours of tinkering with placements on the ground are advisable to fully understand where the critical taper angle starts. Offset Aliens, offset Friends, and the new Black Diamond C3s rule in flaring cracks or pin scars. However, be aware that since most cam angles are about 14 degrees, a cam can't hold at all once the taper angle is 28 degrees or beyond. Another significant problem with tapering cracks is the extra load placed on the cam axles in these placements. A crack with a 14-degree taper will place four times the force on the cam axles, and it only goes up from there.

Camalots (C3s) feature a double axle. The design means the Camalot can cover a significantly larger expansion range than other, comparably sized devices. I will not attempt to describe why this is so. Simply get a unit, fiddle with the movement, and you'll understand the mechanics. The added camming range is also beneficial in flaring cracks, where the disparity of crack width is more pronounced. One drawback of the added range is a slight increase in weight, but technology is making up the difference: The newest Camalots are about 20 percent lighter than the previous generation, with only a slight strength decrease in the components of the larger (.75 and up) sizes. The handle is a durable stainless steel cable. The cams are stamped from aircraft-quality aluminum and are narrower than those found on other SLCDs.

Dirty

All mechanical devices eventually become dirty. For optimal trigger and cam action, clean with soapy water and lubricate with a Teflon or silicone lubricant. Elmer's Slide-All Teflon lubricant is an excellent choice. Do not use oil or oil-based lubricants such as WD40 because they collect dirt, which will eventually gum up the cams, perhaps at the worst possible moment.

Stuck

A stuck SLCD is like seeing a wad of twenty dollar bills lying on the ground that you just can't seem to pick up. But boy do you want to. Once you realize an SLCD might be stuck, be careful how you work with it—frantic jerking can turn a mildly stuck SLCD into a fixed one. As with cleaning any climbing hardware, brute force is a poor removal strategy. Pull hard on the trigger to retract it as far as possible and try to pull the piece straight out. This may seem obvious, but you wouldn't believe how often a novice has claimed an SLCD to be hopelessly stuck, only to have an expert remove it in a few seconds. If that doesn't work, look in the crack for an opening to move the unit through, carefully working the unit toward the edge of the crack. Clever and delicate maneuvering is the best bet for getting the unit free. Some climbers sling the triggers on their SLCDs, particularly the smaller ones, with cord to make removal easier if a unit should get stuck or if the trigger is inside the crack and cannot be reached. As a last resort, clip a sling to this cord with a carabiner and give it a good jerk. If the first tug or two doesn't free the piece, you're usually hosed. Nut tools can often be used to snag the trigger of a stuck SLCD.

This crack is too small for this cam, which is placed with the cams cranked to minimum width. Removal might be difficult. Avoid such placements if at all possible, although in dire circumstances with no other options, it is better to risk losing a cam than losing your life.

SOS

SOS is an acronym devised by Tom Cecil of Seneca Rocks Mountain Guides. It stands for **solid, orientation,** and **surface area.** Beginners often find it helpful to keep SOS in mind when placing most any protection device, especially tapers.

The **S (solid)** tells the climber to check the rock and make sure it is solid, using a sight, sound and feel approach. You first look around (sight) and determine that the rock is of good quality and the area is clear of loose flakes and obvious choss. This helps break the tunnel vision many beginners experience when first learning to place gear. To determine the "sound" aspect, you beat on the rock to see if it's hollow, holding a hand on the rock to feel for vibration. You have to start with solid rock to get a solid primary placement, and climbers should examine the rock in macro and micro terms. In macro terms, what you're looking for is the proverbial straight-in crack set in massive, solid rock, as opposed to a flake crack, or worse, a crack under a block. Micro structure refers to what's inside the crack. Ideally you want a fairly uniform crack devoid of hollow spots, flakes, grit or decomposed sections.

The **O (orientation)** means the placement must be aligned to withstand loading in the anticipated direction of pull. In the event of a fall, you cannot count on the gear holding if it changes direction or must adapt to an oblique angle of pull.

S (surface area) ensures the placement is well seated, with sufficient surface area contacting the rock and everything touching the way you want it. For instance, the most common mistake with SLCDs is that climbers don't look closely at the back cams.

The Stopper placement is flush in this endwise configuration, but how strong is that flake of rock on the right wall of the crack? Probably strong enough to hang off, but not strong enough to hold a leader on a 30-foot ripper. Believe it: The principal cause of anchor failure is rock failure. Protection devices seldom break, but they often rip out, meaning *security,* not strength, is often the main issue. The importance of the "S" in SOS cannot be overstated.

Wild Country offers some specific recommendations for removing stuck cams. First, focus on one pair of cams at a time, and try to feel or see if there is any play. (Wild Country claims the floating trigger design of Friends will enable you to do this, as it allows the manipulation of individual pairs of cams on either side of the axle.) Another solution is to use a pair of bent wires looped around the trigger. Use the loops to fiddle with the trigger while you tap the end of the stem. Another technique is to move or tap the cams sideways, in the direction the axle is pointing (perpendicular to the stem). Finally, don't give up too early, because most cams can be removed with patience.

Investing in Cams

Whenever something is expensive and cherished, there is always someone out there making crude replicas. It's a safe bet that these knockoffs will be inferior to the Real McCoy, even if they look the same. Some of the units look good enough, while others are clearly trash, with loose wires, poor action, wobbly cams, etc. A decade ago knockoff SLCDs were rare but not unheard of. You might have to hunt far and wide to find a shoddy SLCD these days, but understand they might still be out there.

Before buying any SLCD, test the trigger action and the smoothness with which the cams retract and expand. If the cams "wiggle" on the axle, the machining tolerances were not kept tight, which sacrifices the stability of the unit. Bear in mind the age-old saying, "You get what you pay for." In the case of SLCDs, or any climbing gear, buying cheap may land you in the Knotty Pine Motel.

SLIDING NUTS

Many climbers have never owned a sliding nut— and never will. They are currently manufactured on a limited basis. As previously mentioned, the main curse of the sliding nut is the capacity of the unit to seat itself so securely that removal is grim to impossible. Nevertheless, because it is important that you understand the concept of all the protection devices out there, we'll take the time to investigate the sliding nut.

In brief, all sliding nuts work off the principle of opposing wedges. The first examples were simply two tapers arranged on one sling. Next came two cabled tapers, swaged together at the base to form a mutual clip-in loop. On one cable was a taper, right side up; on the other was another taper (or equal size), upside down, which could be

An original sliding nut pair was strung on one cord.

A spring-loaded sliding nut in a virtually perfect placement (one you will rarely get). Note that the symmetry of the crack matches both the fixed taper on the left, and the sliding half-ball component on the right. Likewise, notice that the sliding component is at mid-range on the fixed taper; the unit works best this way. PHOTO BY KEVIN POWELL.

moved up and down the cable. As the two tapers contacted each other, the width of the combined nut increased, eventually fitting the intended placement.

The original slider nuts are long gone. Refinements in the original units have left us with spring-loaded sliding nuts such as Ball Nuts made by CampUSA (formerly Lowe Balls), and ClimbTech Tech Nuts, which employ a boxier shape on the sliding piece. Don't expect the market to become flooded with other sliding nuts. Malcolm Daly, of Trango USA, once informed me that in terms of manufacturing setup, slider nuts are a hassle of the first order. In addition to the manufacturing hardships, slider nuts present some bewildering problems for both the reviewer and the consumer.

Sliding nuts can work like magic, but you must know their limitations. First, sliding nuts are small, especially the smallest ones, which allow placement in the same size cracks as microtapers. Even in ideal placements, the breaking strength of the tiny units is relatively low. Second, the placement is only as good as the purchase of either the cylinder or ball. Because the surface area contacting the rock is pretty small, the rock can sometimes break away if the unit is fallen on. Third, whenever the cylinder or ball is fully extended or at the end of its range, holding power is significantly reduced. Lastly, if the units are placed to hold large loads over sharp edges (a use for which they were not designed), they might hold, but the impact will invariably kink the cable and you'll have to chuck them.

A taper has obvious advantages over the more elaborate sliding nuts in most placements. Most likely, you'll find tapers are stronger, more straightforward to place and remove, and get more surface area on the stone. But in thin, shallow, parallel-sided cracks—and plenty exist—sliding nuts might provide the only option for protection. If you place one on lead, consider placing two and equalizing them, or use a Yates Screamer.

SUMMARY

Selecting your purchase from such a panoply of available protection can be as confusing as throwing down big bucks for a new car. It becomes all the more baffling when you read product catalogs. Most manufacturers are somewhat guilty of overstating their product's capabilities—just the standard business of pimping a product. But we should remember this: The rock-climbing market, though steadily growing, still is relatively small compared to surfing and many other adventure sports. Any product must be viable or it won't last. Almost without exception, all the devices listed here are first-rate in terms of design, materials and construction. Selection, then, is best decided by determining the climbing situations you will most likely encounter, and knowing what gear is specifically suited to them.

This anchor has three solid cams and is well equalized, but the problem is the structural integrity of the rock itself—basically a pile of cracked blocks not well attached to the main formation. How reliable is this anchor? Would the individual pieces fail due to a force exceeding their potential holding power, or would they rip out of the rock because the granite is rotten and the structure weak? Probably the latter. Catastrophic anchor failures occur more often than not from bad rock, pure and simple.

When analyzing rock structure before placing nuts or cams, look at both macro and micro structure. Macro is the big picture. Is the feature a straight-in crack in the planet, or a crack under a car-sized block? Micro is the specifics of the crack itself. Are there any loose flakes or hollow spots inside the crack? Grainy or decomposing rock? Here (an actual field anchor photographed in Joshua Tree), the camming devices are set in suspect rock, basically wedged against a wafer of cracked flakes between the walls of the crack. The whole rig might blow out owing to poor rock quality.

Tapers and camming devices have several standard types, and as the sport evolves, so does the archetypal design. The archetype represents the nut that is best suited for generic use in the United States. When you move too far away from the archetype, you gain advantage in specialized situations, at the loss (though usually limited) of overall utility. With tapers, the standard used to be the straight taper, but now the curved taper is the archetype. A majority of American climbing is done on granite, sandstone or rock that fractures in a similar manner, with reasonably uniform cracks. Hence your basic curved taper is probably best for general use. Not necessarily so in conglomerate rock, where your cutaway or scooped tapers can snag on crystals inside a crack and offer extra holding power.

The four-cam, single center stem SLCD is the archetypal camming device. When you move to the three-cam units, you gain the advantage of lower profile, but one less cam means less surface area on the rock and a reduction, however small, in security.

The point is, all the under-designed gear lacks specific features and has less utility as a generic tool. If much of your climbing is done on rock requiring queer-tailored gear, that's what you should buy. Active local climbers are the best instructors in what gear works best at a given crag. Remember that with the exception of offset tapers, which definitely under-perform a regular taper in parallel-sided cracks, most of the other gear can function almost equally well in a given situation, provided the gear is used by someone who understands its nuances. Fact is, the difference gear makes in your climbing usually is overstated. If you can get one brand of nut to fit, other brands will probably work just as well. That assumes, of course, that the nut is either American or European. American- and European-made products are, by any engineering or manufacturing standards, far superior to all others.

Gear manufacturers now have the option of having their gear tested and CE (Conformité Européenne) certified, and all the top brands do so. All of our strength ratings have so far been discussed in pounds, though in recent years the industry has shifted over to rating everything in kiloNewtons (kN). I've converted everything to pounds for easy comprehension (for Americans), but the time is nigh to deal with kNs as the prevailing system.

In talking with various manufacturers, I came to appreciate the uniqueness of the rock gear business. Not one of the manufacturers sets the top priority on making money (which seems so remarkable that I'm not certain I believe it). Their stated aim is to produce a great product. The understanding, it would seem, is that a good product will result in honorable profits. All talk with deserved pride about their tackle. A hell of a lot of care, passion and engineering creativity is evident in modern rock-climbing hardware, and every climber is indebted to these manufacturers because each has taken our needs so seriously.

There is magnificent parity among all the gear competing for your greenback. Ultimately it's not the gear, but the person placing it that makes the difference. Considering that forty-five years ago, British climbers used to protect their most difficult leads with machine nuts found on the railroad tracks, the present-day climber should respect having such wide choices among what 95 percent of the time is fabulous gear.

Lastly, while we can investigate equipment in a generic way, an active trad climber needs to consider equipment in terms of an ongoing study, much as an attorney is required to take annual courses to keep his license up to date. The trick here is not to try and learn everything at one exhaustive session every year or so, but to casually keep abreast via the gear reviews featured in climbing magazines and on-line analyses. Information is like insurance, and with rock climbing, you want as much as you can get.

Earl Wiggins leads *Place in the Sun,* Garden of the Gods, Colorado. PHOTO BY STEWART M. GREEN.

CHAPTER FOUR

Fixed Gear

One rule of thumb about fixed gear: Never trust it outright. Because it's fixed doesn't mean it will hold a fall, only that it's stuck. One summer a new fixed pin might be so bomber that the Incredible Hulk couldn't clean it with an 8-pound sledge. But after the winter's freeze and thaw, that same pin may be as loose as a tent stake in peat (more on this shortly). Fixed nuts tend to be more reliable, but not always. Remember two things: Somebody probably has tried like the Devil to clean the nut, and its position has probably been compromised. Always check the placement. Since everybody and his brother have tried to clean it, the cable is probably damaged. Fixed micros are almost always abused and worthless. Same goes for SLCDs. Various cleaning widgets and the dread of leaving a $50 to $100 device make fixed SLCDs a rare, but not unseen, occurrence. Usually the cams are rolled so tight you'd need a Sawzall to get the unit out. Still, consider the unit unreliable. The maxim is: Eyeball and test any and all fixed anchors, and presume they are suspect even if they look good. And back them up whenever possible.

PITONS

While pitons no longer have much practical value in free climbing, they are often mandatory tackle for most big walls (though there is currently a clean aid rage going on in Yosemite and other big wall meccas). By and large, the harder the big wall, the more pitoning is required. Knowledge of their use, however, is essential to appreciating their strengths and limitations as fixed anchors.

Piton craft is best left up to the individual to develop—there's really no other way; but several points are worth mentioning. First, common sense is the rule. Use a piton that fits the crack and enters about 75 percent of the way in before you start hammering. Both the spine and the two running edges of the peg should have good bite in the crack, and the peg should ring as you drive it home—like the rising ring of a xylophone. Try to bury it to the hilt, but don't overdrive it, or you'll either never get it out, or ruin it trying to. In soft rock, particularly desert sandstone, you can almost create your own placement by blasting an oversized pin into an undersized crack, but it still might come out with your fingers. Piton use in any rock creates such vile scarring that it is always best to use nuts whenever possible.

There are four basic piton designs. Knifeblades (called Bugaboos in the larger sizes) come in six sizes, from ⅛ to 3/16 inch in width, and from 3 to 4⅞ inches in length. Precision grinding ensures a uniform taper. Lost Arrows (aka horizontals) come in eight sizes, from 5/32 to 9/32 inch in width, and from 1¾ to 4⅝ inches long. Angles come in six sizes, from ½ to 1½ inches. The RURP (Realized Ultimate Reality Piton), a postage stamp–sized peg with a thin, ½-inch-long blade, is for aid only. For merely thin cracks, knifeblades usually work better than RURPs, which come into their own in incipient cracks, where their hatchet-like blades can burrow into the rock.

Piton design has changed little in forty years. The 4130 chrome-moly steel is harder than glacier-polished granite. European imports are generally inferior and rarely seen in the United States. All told, Black Diamond pitons probably are the finest mass-produced line in the world.

The best way to learn piton craft is to grab a handful of pegs, a hammer and aid slings, go to some junky crag where nobody climbs, and experiment low to the ground. Bang in a few, and stand on them to see just how much or how little various placements will hold. After dinking around for a couple of hours, you'll catch on. There's a barbaric joy in slugging steel into the rock, no question about it. Since pitons are rarely used to protect free climbing anymore, the best way to get dialed in is to venture onto a beginning wall climb. Over the course of a dozen or so pitches, you might place and clean one hundred or more pitons, plenty to get a journeyman's feel for the work. Many beginning aid climbers find it helpful to wear glasses of some sort to protect their eyes from the spraying rock fragments that result from errant hammer blows.

Fixed Pitons

I recall the time British ace Ron Fawcett and I were trying to speed climb an aid route on Washington Column in Yosemite. Up in the middle is a left-slanting arch, which at that time bristled with fixed gear. Presuming the gear was all bomber, I never tested anything, or even looked at it; I simply started clipping across it. About 15 feet off the belay, a fixed Angle popped the second I weighted it; Ron was inattentive, dropped me about 25 feet, and I wrenched to a stop with all the hide raked off my knuckles. As this tale illustrates, that fixed piton might look bomber and be no good at all. Again, never trust any fixed gear outright.

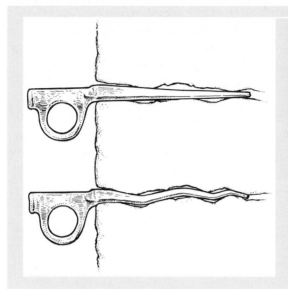

Hard steel pitons (upper) blast their way into a crack, chiseling a tight fit. Soft steel pitons (lower) are still found fixed on many older routes, and work by conforming tightly with the undulations of the crack. Both types of pitons will loosen with weathering and time.

Assuming you have no interest in big walls, have no hammer as you approach a fixed piton belay station, or must rely on fixed pins for lead protection, how do you gauge the security of your anchor? First, inspect the pins. How rusty are they? Do they move? Are they fully driven, or do they hang halfway out of the crack? Are they wee and creaky knifeblades, funky soft steel European pegs, or beefy Lost Arrows or Angles? As with tapers, the bigger the better. Do they cam into a hole in the crack, or will a hard pull likely twist them from their placement? At best, it's still a crapshoot, so back up fixed pins whenever possible.

I can say it again, but many climbers still won't believe that a piece of iron beat into a crack is not necessarily sound. To further prove my point, travel back to Suicide Rock in the early '70s. The name was never more germane than for a young climber from the San Diego area known affectionately as Acapulco Bill, a moniker he earned after a string of spectacular falls that more resembled cliff diving than leader falls. Since Acapulco Bill would only lead, he fell often and far, so far that he had no right to continue on this earth. Somehow he got it in his mind that every fixed pin was solid as Excalibur in situ. Whenever he would spot a fixed pin, he'd slot a quick nut and rush headlong, often running the rope out upwards of 50 feet in his mad quest for some cracked and rusty peg hammered home by John Mendenhall in the '30s. Twice I saw him lunge for such a peg; twice I saw the peg ping out in his hands; and twice I saw Acapulco Bill pitch off for one of his legendary dives. I think it was his wife who finally got him back to the beach and away from the crags.

The reason I mention these stories is that if you venture onto big trad climbs, especially the popular trade routes, fixed pitons are common, unavoidable and often required insofar as they are driven into the only possible placement in a given portion of crack. If you heed the examples we've spelled out here, you'll likely stay out of trouble. Nothing is ever a given with fixed gear.

BOLTS

For more than fifty years, the bolt was the bane of sportsmanlike climbing, though it always played an important role. First ascensionists justified the judicious bolt, but routinely risked much and scared themselves stiff to avoid placing it. The attitudes of sport climbing have changed all that, and presently the majority of the most notorious routes are predominantly, if not entirely, bolt protected. The bold runout is, for the most part, a relic of the past. Since bolts now play such a leading role in current climbing—at all levels—it's best we go into some detail about them.

Bolt History

Before the early 1980s, no company manufactured bolts specifically designed for climbing, leaving folks to rummage through the local hardware store for whatever might work as a rock anchor. Some climbers researched the subject, checking manufacturer guidelines and specs for tension (straight out pull) and shear strength, going with the best they could find or, in some cases, whatever was on sale. These bolts were devised as hardware fasteners and construction anchors for concrete, block, brick and stone. Because there were many varieties of these bolts, if you should ever climb an old, obscure route in a seldom-visited area, you might clamber upon some curious, seldom-seen and almost certainly rickety bolts. On well-traveled routes, local activists have generally replaced the old construction items with bomber, made-for-climbing bolts, hangers and anchor setups.

The ubiquitous hex-head 5-piece Rawl bolt. Somewhat of a standard, this is probably the most common bolt you'll encounter, now sold under the brand name Powers Bolt. In a good placement the hanger should snug up flush and flat against the wall. A 5-piece Rawl actually has 6 pieces. In solid granite the ⅜-inch diameter rates at over 7,000 pounds shear strength and almost 5,000 pounds pullout strength.

Manufacturer strength ratings are gauged for the bolt being placed in cement. Since the density of concrete varies, there's usually a chart giving strength ratings in pounds per square inch (PSI) for a bolt placed in different concrete densities, for example, 3000 PSI, 4000 PSI, 5000 PSI, etc. With 3000 PSI cement, it would take a 3,000-pound block to crush it. The hardest, fine-grained granite is probably the equivalent of 4000 to 5000 PSI concrete. To simplify our discussion, all strength ratings given here are based on bolts placed in 4000 PSI concrete, roughly equivalent to medium- to hard-density rock. Softer rock, like desert sandstone, would probably fall in the 0 to 2000 PSI range.

Back in the 1950s, though, the Star Dryvin bolt was the norm for use as a rock-climbing anchor. Star Dryvins were wedge-type hammer-ins, and can infrequently still be found on classic climbs in Yosemite, Tahquitz, the Tetons and a host of other areas. In the desert, many climbers preferred to bang in a ½-inch baby angle piton into a ⅜-inch drilled hole, rather than use one of the hardware store bolts. A ½-inch baby angle slugged into a ⅜-inch hole has been tested at an average of 3,500 pounds (shear strength), provided the eye of the pin is pointed down and the hole drilled at a slight downward angle. Pullout strength is only about 1,000 pounds, however.

Anyway, for twenty years, the bolt of choice was the Star Dryvin, which used a lead sleeve and a steel nail. The sleeve was tapped into the hand-drilled hole, then the nail was hammered home, spreading the sleeve. In even the best rock, and in the larger ⅜-inch size, the shear strength of these bolts was little more than 1,000 pounds, and they'd pull out with far less force. If you should ever come across an antique bolt with a star-shaped icon on the nailed head—beware. You've just found the climbing equivalent of an arrowhead. Even when newly placed—and that was many decades ago—Star Dryvins were iffy. Climbers in the know will remove the bolt on the spot, bagging a genuine relic for their one-bolt museum.

Another vintage, rarely seen and altogether lousy bolt for a climbing anchor was the infamous Rawl Zamac Nailin. These duds look much like the ¼-inch Rawl Drive buttonhead, save for the center pin/nail in the middle of the buttonhead, which is hammered flush to the buttonhead during installation. On its best day in Yosemite granite a Zamac would shear off under a 1,500-pound load and would pull out with half as much poundage. The challenging Yosemite slab route, *Shaky Flakes,* had many of these Zamac nails protecting long, 5.10+ runouts, and worse still, the topo in the 1987 *Yosemite Climbs* guidebook noted that pitch 6 featured a "rivet belay," which is like tying off a quarter horse to a whippoorwill. These "coffin

A relic from the old days, this ¼-inch Rawl Drive buttonhead still looks good after twenty-five years; the stainless steel hanger shows no signs of corrosion. In trad climbing areas most aging, ¼-inch bolts have been replaced, but you'll still find some on more obscure climbs, stuck in the stone like slow-ticking time bombs. In fine-grained, iron-hard granite, one of these contraction bolts *might* hold 2,000 pounds. In anything less than perfect rock, old Rawl buttonheads should never be trusted. Here the placement looks acceptable: The bolt is perpendicular to the plane of the rock face, and the head of the bolt and hanger is flush to the rock. What can't be judged by visual inspection is the length of the bolt. These ¼ buttonheads come in lengths ranging from ¾ inch to 1½ inches. I've replaced dozens of these ¼-inch bolts over the years. Many were removed simply by putting a claw hammer behind the hanger and prying outward, with about the same force required to pull a nail from a piece of particleboard.

nails" have long since been replaced, but heads up if you venture onto obscure routes established in the sixties or early seventies. You might get Zamaced.

In the sixties, most climbers changed over to the ¼-inch Rawl Drive, hammer-in contraction bolt, though some pioneers (the legendary Fred Beckey among them) sometimes used the dinky ³⁄₁₆-inch-diameter device. The Rawl Drive hammer-in featured a split shank that was squeezed together when banged into the narrow hole. The outward spring force against the walls of the hole kept the bolt snug—for a while. These bolts came in both buttonhead and screw-top styles, the latter being weaker because of the threads. When newly placed, the shear strength of the ¼-inch-diameter Rawl Drive was only about 2,200 pounds, while the pullout strength, especially in soft rock, was in the low 100s, if even that high. A liability for the threaded version was that the threads could get stripped during placement. If the threads do not extend above the nut once the nut has been tightened, the bolt is basically worthless. (Such a bolt failed and killed two climbers ascending fixed lines on Yosemite's Glacier Point Apron. The route was later named *Anchors Away*.) For nearly twenty years, though, these contraction bolts were used without question and were employed easily five to one over all other designs.

While the ¼-inch Rawl was by far the most popular bolt, some climbers switched over to the ⁵⁄₁₆- and ³⁄₈-inch-diameter sizes. These larger sizes were still possible to hand drill and were vastly stronger—in both shear and pullout strength— than the ¼-inch-diameter model. The ⁵⁄₁₆-inch-diameter Rawl Drive buttonhead had a shear strength of about 4,800 pounds, and in hard granite, for a time became the hand-drilled bolt of choice of many ground-up first ascensionists. Unfortunately the 5⁄16-inch-diameter Rawl Drive was discontinued. Although there was still the 3⁄8-inch-diameter model, with a titanic shear strength approaching 7,500 pounds (in perfect granite), few climbers were willing to hand drill a 3⁄8-inch-diameter hole 2 inches deep while balanced on a crumbling rugosity, so they appeared more often as rappel and anchor bolts. For lead protection, the 1⁄4-inch Rawl still reigned.

Only after about ten years did the abundant shortcomings of the 1⁄4-inch Rawl Drive come to light. First, contraction bolts are under constant pressure. Given time, that pressure decreases and the bolt's outward-spring force becomes far less; thus the bolt can creep from the hole as the tension relaxes. Radical changes in temperatures—sweltering summers and freezing winters—hasten the process. Second, the metal is prone to corrosion, the rate of corrosion being tied to the mineral content of the rock. In fact all non-stainless steel bolts eventually rust. Improper placement, crooked or oblique holes, weakening through hammer blows and a slew of other problems make even a perfectly set 1⁄4-inch contraction bolt a liability after only a few seasons. Lastly, it takes considerable resistance to fully depress the bolt's split shank, something impossible in softer rock like sandstone or quartz monzonite. More often than not, Rawl Drive bolts placed in soft rock deform the hole and never accomplish the requisite outward-spring tension needed to make them even remotely adequate as an anchor. Even the 3⁄8-inch-diameter Rawl Drive, when tested in soft rock, exhibited pullout strengths of between 500 and 1,000 pounds—unacceptable by any measure. Consequently, you should not trust a 1⁄4-inch contraction bolt in softer rock, even if it's been placed recently.

Behold the woeful "spinner," when a bolt (like this) protrudes from the hole and the hanger is not flush against the rock. The hole was not drilled deep enough, and when hammered in, the shaft bottomed out in the back of the hole, preventing the head of the bolt from pinning the hanger flush against the rock.

Amazingly, this bolt shows virtually no signs of corrosion after thirty years at Joshua Tree. Stainless steel has become the standard for bolts and hangers as it protects against corrosion, although many carbon steel bolts are used because they are less expensive.

Considering that the Rawl Drive bolts were originally designed as temporary masonry anchors, it's amazing they were largely functional for so many years. Why more of these ¼-inch contraction bolts have not failed is one of climbing's great mysteries. Just how poor many of them have become was never better illustrated than when several local Suicide and Tahquitz climbers set out to replace all the old bolts in the Idyllwild climbing areas. Recall that before the sticky boot revolution of the early 1980s, the harder climbs at Suicide were much sought after, and many teams spent whole afternoons "falling up" them. Yet bolts that had held literally thousands of falls often were removed with a single hammer blow. Many were yanked out with a claw hammer with about the same effort needed to clean a nail from plywood. The message here is that extreme care should be used before trusting old contraction bolts. Though they were strong enough initially, time has drastically reduced their strength. Again, these bolts were designed not for rock climbing, but as lightweight industrial anchors for concrete and masonry, and they usually had served their intended purpose after a few weeks or months. They were never meant to act as the point from which a person's life could hang, nor for decades of such use. If you do have to clip a sketchy ¼-inch bolt for lead pro, use a Yates Screamer, back it up if possible and don't fall.

Even worse than ¼-inch bolts are ¼-inch bolts with no hangers. Doubtless some blockhead pilfered the hanger and left you at the headwaters of Shit Creek. If you must climb this route (as opposed to going down, which should always be an option if the anchors are bogus), the best trick is to slide the head down on a smaller-sized wired taper, slip the newly exposed loop of cable over the stud and cinch the head tight against the stud. Hopefully the stud still has a nut to hold the taper cable on; otherwise the placement is good only for aid. Even with a nut, this dicey connection to the bolt will not hold any outward pull, so don't fall.

There was a scandal approximately fifteen years ago when some distributors from hell were counterfeiting inferior bolts made from low-grade materials instead of the stronger alloys specified for anchors. It is not inconceivable that this type of alarming profiteering still occurs on occasion. While modern bolts have taken tons (literally) of abuse with few mishaps, no single anchor, bolt or chock should be considered 100 percent reliable. Backups are essential, especially for belay and rappel anchors. Among the most dangerous times of a lead is the beginning of a pitch or just above a ledge, where few bolts or chocks separate the leader from the ground or ledge. To make matters worse, the impact force a leader can generate is greatest early in the pitch, when only a small amount of rope is available to absorb the shock of the fall.

In the early eighties, when climbers first started using something other than Rawl contraction bolts, the USE Diamond Taper Bolt gained momentary popularity. The required hole was routine to drill, but the Taper Bolt tests were inconsistent. When testing for straight out pull, half the bolts tested to 3,000 pounds, while the other half failed on average at a measly 700 pounds. This push-type bolt is installed by screwing the tapered, threaded section into a lead sleeve, expanding the sleeve outward. Installation is straightforward, but the Taper Bolt is very tricky to place correctly. Inserting and hammering on the bolt easily mauls the lead sleeve. The gap between the head of the bolt and the rock must be judged exactly prior to torquing, because a specific number of turns are required for full strength. One turn too few seriously decreases its holding power, and one turn too many can strip the lead sleeve, rendering the bolt useless. Even climbers experienced with the Taper Bolt often botched placement, and worse yet, a poorly placed Taper Bolt is hard to detect without a crowbar. With only the ability to visually inspect the bolt, consider all Taper Bolts—especially the ¼-inch-diameter units—to be suspect. Long ago the Taper Bolt fell out of favor; it is not recommended and should be used with extreme caution when found on a route. To identify a Taper Bolt, look for the letters "USE" on the hex-shaped bolt head.

In the mid-1980s, when sport climbing and rappel bolting took over the U.S. climbing scene, the quality of bolts drastically changed for the better. Modern sport-climbing routes do not feature the old-style Rawl Drive bolts, or any bolt of ¼-inch diameter. The modern standard calls for expansion bolts of ⅜ to ½ inch diameter. The Rawl 5-piece and Rawl Stud were the most popular bolts in the United States throughout the eighties and nineties. The Rawl 5-piece is a "pullout" type bolt that pulls a cone into an expanding sleeve by cranking on the bolt head with a wrench. The Rawl 5-piece (now sold under the brand name Powers Bolt) is one of the best rock bolts available. It has good strength (7,900 pounds shear strength for the ⅜ inch), is suitable for a variety of rock surfaces and is relatively

This ⅜-inch threaded Rawl bolt looks perfectly set in great rock—good to go.

foolproof to install. For full-strength protection, the Rawl bolt is torqued to about 35 foot-pounds for the ⅜ incher, and 60 foot-pounds for the ½-inch model. Modest cost, availability, straightforward installation and general reliability has made the Rawl 5-piece the bolt of choice.

The Rawl Stud also pulls a cone into an expanding sleeve, but in this case only when a nut is tightened on the threaded bolt. A ⅜- by 2-inch Rawl Stud has a shear strength of 5,420 pounds and a pullout strength of 4,310 pounds. While not quite as strong as the Rawl 5-piece, owing to the threads on the bolt, the Rawl Stud is quicker and easier to place for those few remaining mavericks who do their bolting on lead and only have one hand to place and tighten the bolt (the other hand is hanging on to the holds). Over the last decade Petzl, Fixe, Raumer and other companies have started making bolts specifically for rock climbing, and the 5-piece Rawl has not only stood the test of time, it seems to be as good as all the others.

We purposefully have neglected the business of how to place bolts. Establishing routes that require bolts traditionally has been, and should remain, in the realm of the expert, and therefore is beyond the scope of this book. If you do place bolts, make sure you take the time to learn their proper use, as the lives of others will ride on your craftsmanship. More than one person has hit the deck because of another's sloppy work. For those community service–minded individuals who replace aging and dangerous bolts, the standard is stainless steel for hangers, bolts, chains, anchor links and ring hardware. By using stainless throughout, problems with galvanic and stress corrosion are nearly eliminated in all but the most corrosive saltwater environments. For more information on this subject, a good place to start is the American Safe Climbing Association (ASCA) Web site at www.safeclimbing.org.

Bolt Hangers

With the rise in popularity of sport climbing has come a slew of new bolt hanger designs. Any of the commercially available hangers are certain to meet the specs required for the situation. Aluminum hangers, homemade or otherwise, should be considered suspect if they have taken repeated high-force falls. Always eyeball

This ¼-inch buttonhead is installed using the infamous "SMC Death Hanger," a moniker that stuck after several such hangers failed under body weight (possibly due to a stress corrosion problem) on Yosemite's Middle Cathedral Rock. The hanger has taken on a distinctly bronze tint. NOT to be trusted.

These hangers were recalled long ago by Ed Leeper due to stress corrosion problems. Though unreliable, many such hangers are still out there, especially in classic trad areas. These hangers should be replaced and upgraded to stainless steel, as should all ¼-inch bolts.

A ⅜-inch 5-piece Rawl with a Metolius hanger. Somebody painted it to match the rock, but the paint is chipping off. Factory-painted bolts fare much better.

suspect hangers for cracks or other deformation. Stainless steel is the material of choice. The old-style SMC hanger is a relic from the seventies and early eighties that had significant stress/galvanic corrosion problems rendering them untrustworthy. This hanger is readily identifiable by its dull yellow brown tint. It is somewhat thinner (slightly thinner than a quarter) than the newer, thicker and totally bomber stainless steel hangers that after many years still retain their high sheen with little sign of corrosion. Another hanger to watch out for is the infamous Leeper hanger, manufactured and now recalled (due to stress corrosion problems) by Ed Leeper. These are easy to spot owing to their badly rusted condition and trapezoidal shape.

Metolius and Fixe have led the current trend to minimize the visual impact of fixed anchors by offering camouflaged stainless steel hangers. If not using these, responsible first ascensionists often paint their hangers to match the color of the rock. Petzl and Raumer also make excellent hangers, along with a handful of other companies.

Homemade hangers are seldom seen, but they are out there and run the gamut from sawed off and drilled angle iron to double links of chain. Some are good, some are bad—it's your guess. Some of the older homemades, nicknamed "pop-offs," feature a design that twists the downward pull of a falling climber into an outward pull on the bolt stud, which could prove disastrous with an old ¼-inch contraction bolt. Beware of any hanger that levers the bolt outward.

Now and in the Future

Cost is the only reason not to use stainless steel bolt hardware. Carbon steel bolts cost about a third of what you pay for the stainless article. Carbon steel 5-piece Rawls have shown considerable corrosion after only ten years, and even in dry desert climates like Joshua Tree. If you're going to take on the responsibility of replacing old bolts, or installing new ones on first ascents, strongly consider using

While over twenty years old, this threaded Rawl bolt and stainless steel SMC hanger still look good. The rock is solid desert granite, the placement is perpendicular and the hanger is flush. Every twenty-year-old bolt should look so good.

stainless steel. Many companies (and the ASCA) will donate the requisite stainless bolts and hardware to those willing to spend the time and effort to upgrade old hardware.

For sea cliffs, even stainless steel bolts and hangers have shown rapid stress corrosion; in Thailand, for example, many old bolts have failed under body weight. The solution might be a single, glue-in titanium bolt. Ushba makes a corrosion-resistant, 10mm titanium ring bolt called the Tortuga, rated at 5,620 pounds. While expensive, everything else has so far failed over the short haul.

WHAT TO DO WITH THAT BOLT . . .

There is no absolutely reliable method to test in-situ bolts, but there are plenty of reasons to want to. Here are some suggestions:

Always consider a ¼-inch bolt suspect. They haven't been placed as anchors for over two decades, though they are still found on older routes.

Make sure the bolt hanger is flush to the wall and not a "spinner," where the hanger spins freely on the stud. A spinner indicates the hole was drilled too shallow for the bolt stud, or that the bolt stud has crept out from the hole, which happens with contraction bolts. And don't try to fix the spinner by hammering on it. Had that been possible, the first party would have sunk it. Further hammering can only damage the shank and the head.

Keep an eye out for cratering, which occurs in brittle or extremely hard rock, and is usually the result of sloppy drilling, which forms a chipped-away crater around the hole. Cratering can greatly reduce the bolt's purchase because the rock surrounding the shank is damaged.

Check the hanger for cracks.

If the bolt is a screwhead, make sure the nut is snug and the threads are in good shape. I learned this after taking a 30-foot grounder (into a snowbank, luckily) when the hanger popped off the denuded threads of such a bolt. If the bolt is a buttonhead, or looks like a machine bolt, again make sure it's snugly set and free of fatigue cracks.

If the bolt is clearly bent, or looks to be set in an oblique hole, beware!

Discoloration is natural enough, but excessive rust denotes a so-called coffin nail. Use common sense. If the bolt looks funky, don't trust it. And always back up bolts (that don't meet the modern standard) with a nut, if possible. A perfect bolt is nearly impossible to pull out, even with an astronomical fall, but there are a lot of bolts out there that are something less than perfect. Better safe than splattered.

COLD SHUTS

A trend at some sport-climbing areas is to use construction cold shuts (hooks)—either open, closed or welded—for hangers. Cold shuts used in climbing are generally borrowed from heavy construction work, where by and large they are used for anchoring, as well as interim links connecting two large chains. (The cold shut is slid between the end links of two chains and is then beaten "shut," thus connecting the chain.) Because said chains are often hauling around mambo industrial loads, the larger shuts are usually quite strong—some test-rated to upwards of 3,000 pounds. However, because cold shuts are borrowed from construction, they are not UIAA-tested or approved. While they may, or may not, meet established climbing standards in terms of strength, they have been a staple in California climbing for over fifteen years, and to a lesser extent, at many other sport-climbing areas.

Even the strongest shuts are not used as protection, rather they are doubled up at the top of clip-and-go sport routes and serve as fixed anchors for the leader to lower and then to toprope other climbers wanting to follow, but not lead, the route. One handy feature of cold shuts is their relatively large diameter and rounded surface, which allows the rope to be placed directly through the hanger for lowering. When two open cold shuts are fixed at the tops of some routes, at the end of the climb, you simply drape the rope through the open shuts and lower off. Though some people still swear by them, others are leery to toprope off such hangers. Closed cold shuts may be adequate for lowering and toproping situations, but are not up to snuff for lead protection.

Welded cold shuts are available that meet the standard for lead climbing, lowering and toproping. Reportedly, it's slightly easier for a quickdraw to accidentally unclip from a welded cold shut than from a traditional hanger, but the cold shut offers easy retreat from any point on the route, and it's easier on carabiners.

This welded steel cold shut shows signs of corrosion just a few years after installation. Many manufacturers (such as FIXE) now offer the preferable stainless steel cold shuts. While more expensive, they'll most likely last a lifetime.

Convenience has made cold shuts popular top anchors on routes that see massive traffic, especially so on sport climbs that people "lap" for workout purposes. The problem is that with all those ropes running through the shuts, coupled with the abrasion caused when lowering, a beefy cold shut can, after a few seasons (or less), thin to the breadth of a paper clip. Once a shut is visibly grooved, its holding power is significantly reduced and its temper shot from so much heating and cooling. Inspect shuts for wear and tear and avoid those that are clearly eroded from use. I've seen some shuts in Malibu State Park (a popular sport crag in Southern California) that were worn almost entirely through. Locals usually replace shuts on trade routes, but not always, so keep your eyes open and don't trust the well-worn shuts. If and when you come across sketchy shuts, you might have to climb down to the last protection and lower off from there. Do whatever is necessary to avoid trusting untrustworthy gear. And use quickdraws whenever toproping off cold shuts.

That much said, Fixe and Raumer (distributed by Climb High) now sell a variety of sport-climbing hardware including stainless steel cold shuts, sport anchors and ring anchors that will last far longer than the hardware store variety aluminum and steel cold shuts described above.

WEBBING (SLING MATERIAL)

One of my first climbing outings was to Suicide Rock in Idyllwild, California—in winter. Rick Accomazzo and I spent two hours post-holing through hip-deep snowdrifts just getting to the crag, which had a 30-foot snow cone at its base—a boon, we reckoned, since the top of the cone put us above the crux lower moves of several then-prestigious routes. Ricky roped up, front-pointed up the snow cone and went to work on *Frustration*. He got about 10 feet up a hinging lieback and set a nut, his wet boots skedaddling all over the place. Two moves higher, he popped, the 1-inch sling on the nut broke, and Ricky, poor fellow, slammed into and through the crust of the hollow snow cone, leaving behind a perfect sketch of his corpus, the kind detectives chalk around a slain thug on the tarmac. By the time Ricky had clawed his way out of the hole, his fingers were so numb that for two weeks afterwards he had to use his thumbs to take a leak. Our mistake was to string a nut with a sling we'd filched off a rappel anchor out at Joshua Tree. Who knows how old it was, or how it had been abused. Never again.

On the other hand, a climbing magazine ran a test some years back, where they filched several dozen slings left from popular rappel points on trade routes in Yosemite Valley. They repeatedly found that even when the slings were badly burned from ropes being pulled through them (to retrieve the ropes after rappel), or were sun bleached nearly white, four of these slings (no matter which ones), when combined, held loads exceeding 2,500 pounds, loads almost never encountered in climbing.

What these two anecdotes tell us is that old slings can respond to loading in unpredictable and surprising ways, whereas new slings are not only comparatively inexpensive, but predictably stout.

Slings that are 1, ⅝, and 9/16 inch in width are routinely used in anchor setups, as tie-ins, for equalizing two or more separate anchors, and for connecting ropes to trees, flakes, tunnels and other natural rock features. Dyneema (Dyneema, Spectra and Dynex are all the same thing) is currently favored over other so-called tech-webbing materials. Nevertheless, a brief overview is in order.

A Little Webbing History

Since World War II, nylon webbing has been widely used in rock climbing. Invented to batten down gear on PT Boats, climbers have found nylon webbing (flat rope or "tape") useful as gear slings, runners and tie-offs. Later, several wraps of the 1- or 2-inch variety came to form the swami belt, the standard tie-in device (a harness of sorts) for more than twenty years. As of about 1980, formal harnesses—feather light and heroically strong—replaced the old swami belts, and webbing presently is used almost exclusively as sling material.

Left: 1-inch mil-spec nylon webbing. Right: 9/16-inch Blue Water Spectra high-tech webbing. PHOTO BY JOHN BURBIDGE.

For fifty years standard nylon webbing was used to form slings of 1 and 9/16 inch diameter, the latter for tying off pitons. The ⅝-inch sling was introduced about twenty-five years ago. The strength of the material was more than adequate for its applications. The shortcomings of pure nylon, however, are that it weakens with age and use, and as is the case with all webbing, it is adversely affected by exposure to sunlight's ultraviolet rays.

The great majority of nylon webbing is manufactured for the military, and the government has set minimum requirements, or specs, that the webbing must meet for use in life-support situations. Mil-spec simply refers to these government or military specifications. Fifteen years ago, Blue Water went several steps further than the minimum mil-specs to produce their outstanding Climb-Spec webbing.

The standard mil-spec webbing has a corduroy-type finish because of the many small ridges in the weave. Climb-Spec has refined this weave, eliminating the ridges to produce a "sateen" finish, which is essentially flat and smooth to the touch. This new weave affords two significant advantages: First, it allows a greater density of nylon thread, increasing the strength (of 1-inch webbing) some 500 pounds; second, and more importantly, it increases the wear-resistance upwards of 50 percent. Blue Water Climb-Spec is available in both 1 and 9/16 inch, and comes in bulk form or pre-sewn runners. The 1-inch sling tests out at 7,400 pounds (some 2,000 pounds higher than standard webbing), while the 9/16 inch is good to 4,500 pounds.

Though nylon is still a viable, sometimes preferable, material for slings, other materials have come to replace it in some situations. Blue Water's Spectra is a molecular-weight polyethylene developed by Allied-Signal, Inc. It is the strongest fiber ever made. Pound-for-pound, it is ten times stronger than steel. It is also about ten times as expensive. Spectra-sewn runners are available in various sizes and are for those who want half the bulk and weight of other runners with no significant reduction in strength. According to Bill Griggers of Blue Water, the company doesn't manufacture 1-inch Spectra slings because the cost would be prohibitive and 12,000-pound test webbing is absurd overkill. Spectra's wear resistance is excellent. When cut, Spectra will not tear through. Spectra was for a time the sling of choice throughout the United States. However Dyneema (which the engineers at Black Diamond assure me is essentially the same thing as Spectra), also manufactured by Allied Signal, has come to replace Spectra as the favored sling material. Dyneema is fifteen times stronger than steel. It's now available in 8mm width as the standard size.

Aside from the price, Spectra/Dyneema do have shortcomings. They can be up to 19 percent less resistant to UV damage than regular mil-spec nylon, and too slick to work as well as nylon for the friction knots used in self-rescue situations (prusik knot, Klemheist, etc.). They weaken when repeatedly flexed under moderate loads, whereas nylon does not. In fact, after about 200 flex cycles with a 40-pound load, a Spectra sling is no stronger than a nylon one, and only gets weaker with more flexing. They also have a low melting temperature, so a rope running across can burn them easily. They do not stretch at all, which can also cause them to heat up when directly weighted in a dynamic fall situation. Spectra/Dyneema can actually be weaker than standard nylon webbing under these conditions, because standard webbing will stretch. In this sense the biggest strength of these super fibers is also their biggest weakness. As we will discuss later, the reliability of anchors and the overall safety system depends on the dynamic qualities of the components to slow down the loading curve so peak loading doesn't occur all at once. Imagine tying a double boot to end A of a stout rubber band, and another double boot to end A of a shoestring. If you were to drop both boots from the same height while holding the B ends of the rubber band and shoestring, which double boot would provide the bigger and more sudden loading? This is an exaggerated contrast of stretchy nylon and no-stretch Spectra and high-tensile cord, but understand that in some cases, stronger material can actually result in a less secure overall system.

Despite the drawbacks of these new fibers, and others like them, many climbers consider them superior to standard mil-spec nylon for use as sling material. However, mil-spec runners also have some drawbacks of their own. There have been isolated cases of mil-spec runners tearing over razor-sharp edges. And nylon does wear out, so it is not unheard of for old runners to break under the impact of a fall. But I have never heard of a nylon sling in good condition breaking when the system has been properly rigged. Consequently the far cheaper mil-spec webbing remains a viable, and in some cases, a favored choice for slings—provided the climber keeps a sharp eye on their condition and retires them when signs of wear are obvious. If the nylon feels stiff, it probably has been affected by sunlight—but the webbing may be weakened and show no such sign. If there is any doubt, retire your runners after using them for a period of, say, one hundred days, remembering that the relatively inexpensive nylon is far less precious than your life.

Sewn webbing loops are stronger, lighter and less bulky than knotted ones, so most climbers usually use sewn slings. Nylon slings equipped with a water knot can come in handy for tying around trees, flakes and tunnels in the event of a retreat, but you should check the water knots frequently, as they have a tendency to come untied.

Short, sewn loops of webbing called quickdraws are one of the principal uses of webbing these days. Quickdraws are mandatory equipment for clipping the lead rope into bolts and chocks; they prevent rope drag and decrease the likelihood that the rope will wiggle a chock out of its placement.

Sling material is always in the process of being improved as new manufacturing techniques and textiles become available. In today's world of technology, even the most popular and field-tested gear remains the same for only a matter of years before something better comes along. So as with all other climbing gear, sling material requires on-going study to keep abreast of leading technology. The other option is to simply go with low-tech, inexpensive, time-proven nylon, which in some essential ways is just as good, and sometimes far better, than the space-age item.

HIGH TECH VS. NYLON

Recent testing strongly suggests that old-style nylon sling material (and cordage) is superior for general use in rock climbing. The mega-strong "tech webbings" (such as Spectra/Dyneema materials) were originally produced for the military, generally for securing static loads. Static forces in climbing are basically body-weight loads, far too small to require sling material "stronger than steel." More importantly, in a climbing context, the strength of sling materials is significant only during falls, when dynamic, not static, forces are generated. Since climbing's roped safety system acts as a peak (dynamic) force load limiter, nylon with just a little bit of stretch helps to absorb peak forces, while the virtually static tech webbing translates dynamic forces directly to the carabiners and protection devices, which can blow apart under high-impact dynamic loading. Moreover, recent tests from several sources indicate that nylon webbing and cordage can absorb (without breaking) greater dynamic forces than high-tensile strength cord and tech webbing.

CORDAGE

Accessory cord comes in several styles made from different materials. In the old days cordage was used to sling hexes and nuts; now those products come equipped with wire cables, and cordage is mostly used to fashion cordelettes and prusiks. It comes in a range of diameters up to 9mm and can be bought in any length desired, custom cut off a spool at your local climbing store.

The differences between standard nylon accessory cord (aka utility cord) and newer high-tensile cords (such as New England Ropes' Tech Cord and Blue Water's Titan Spectra cord) are fairly simple to sort out. Nylon stretches a small amount because it's made strictly of nylon; the newer cords combine materials such as Aramid, Dyneema and Technora with nylon. They do not stretch as much as nylon, if at all. The newer cords are lighter, less bulky and, most importantly, stronger—but this strength advantage can be lost depending on which knot is used (up to 40 percent loss of strength on high tensile with a figure eight knot), whereas knotted nylon hardly loses any strength at all.

Which cord works best for what situation is a matter of some debate, but the most up-to-date thinking recommends 7mm nylon, with its attending stretch, for use in rigging cordelettes. The increased stretch equals decreased force on the anchor, meaning more security in the event of a fall.

As far as knots go, it is generally accepted that a double fisherman's knot is sufficient for nylon cord, while a triple fisherman's knot is best for high-tensile cord.

Note that Black Diamond no longer makes Gemini cord. They now distribute Beal 5.5 Aramid and Beal 5.5 Dyneema cord. Kevlar cord is no longer on the market.

Climbers on *Butterballs*, Yosemite, California. PHOTO BY BOB GAINES.

CHAPTER FIVE

Fall Forces and the Jesus Nut

Gear manufacturers are required to have their equipment independently tested and certified before releasing their product to the climbing public, at least in Europe, the biggest market. Manufacturers also test their own and everyone else's product in the hopes of gaining a competitive edge in the market. The bulk of these tests establish the strength of this carabiner or that sling. For better or worse, such testing has provided much of our statistical knowledge about the static and dynamic forces involved in climbing's roped safety system.

In terms of influencing rigging and anchor-building strategies, the lab-simulated factor 2 fall has for decades been the most important and definitive test. The test was originally devised to measure the number of severe falls a climbing rope would hold and the maximum force it would impart to a falling climber. To that end, an 80-kilo iron block (about 175 pounds, the weight of an average climber) is lashed to the end of a 2.8-meter (9-foot) length of rope. The other end of the rope is tied off to a fixed anchor (usually an inflexible iron bolt). The tie-offs for both the iron block and the anchor use .3 meters of rope. The iron climber is hoisted 2.5 meters above the anchor point and dropped through midair for a total free fall of 5 meters.

Experts always agreed that this drop test produced the greatest peak force that could ever be encountered in any fall on a rope, because the fall distance is twice (factor 2) the length of the rope available to absorb energy. Possibly because it was called a *simulated* drop test, the common understanding was that the test replicated a real life, on-the-rock, factor 2 fall and provided legitimate evaluations of forces on that account. Consequently a factor 2 fall, and the forces measured in the lab drop test, became the Gold Standard by which all anchors were measured.

This climber needs to set a Jesus Nut—fast. Even with that, this anchor is sketchy. The idea that two wee nuts in a seam constitute a viable anchor is an idea that will make you dead. Even if the belayer had equalized the nuts with a sliding X, they are still not nearly enough. And since there is no oppositional nut, this anchor is worthless for an upward pull, which is the only direction the pull will come from once the first nut is in place. If the leader were to fall here—which he looks close to doing—the impact would rip the anchor right out (provided the belayer's hip belay could hold such a fall, which is questionable), and the two dupes would shortly find themselves in the Golden City, harps in hand, wondering what went wrong.
PHOTO BY KEVIN POWELL.

From Chamonix to Katmandu, a belay was not "good enough" if it couldn't withstand the forces that the drop test said were generated during a factor 2 test fall.

To appreciate those forces, and what they mean to a climber placing protection and building anchors, you need to know the system used in the lab tests to measure those forces. This is a bit confusing for Americans (who are still using their own private measuring systems) because the lab testing is conducted using the metric system. Here mass is expressed in kilograms, and force (the consequence of mass accelerating or decelerating) is expressed in units called Newtons. Weight, mass and force are all different things; Americans express forces encountered in climbing's roped safety system in terms of pounds of force (lbf). One pound-force is about 4.44 Newtons. One thousand Newtons equals one kiloNewton (kN), a common value in climbing testing and product specifications. *To get a quick conversion, simply remember that 1 kN is basically 225 lbf.*

While a physicist might chuckle at this simplification of a complex and nuanced subject, we need only understand things in terms of simple values since it's the roped safety system, not the derived figures, that is our mortal concern.

FORCES FACTS

- Essential peak (dynamic) force load-limiter qualities in the belay system depend on flex and give in the components.

- Flex and give in the belay system keep dynamic forces of a real world factor 2 fall lower than forces recorded in the lab during a "simulated factor 2 fall drop test."

- The top piece always absorbs the greatest force during a fall, therefore *the top piece is the most important component in the entire belay chain*—be it a point of protection, or the belay anchor itself.

- Make certain, so far as humanly possible, that the top piece of pro, and not the belay anchor, arrests any and all leader falls.

- The main task of the belay is to limit loading on the topmost protection.

- The most critical time is when a leader is first leaving the belay and has yet to place the first piece of protection (the Jesus Nut).

- The belay anchor is not completed, and the roped safety system is not truly online, till a secure Jesus Nut is placed.

STATIC AND DYNAMIC FORCES

Imagine a leader hanging off a bolt on an overhanging sport climb. The force on the bolt will equal the climber's weight, and that weight is a static force because all the objects in the overall system are at rest. Static force loading is what you have all over your house. That nail in the wall on which your Picasso hangs is sustaining the weight, or static force, of Pablo's painting. Your desk sustains the static force of your computer. Your chair sustains the static force of your body.

In climbing, dynamic force occurs when a climber's body speeds up during a fall and slows down when she is arrested by the belay. Dynamic forces quickly build to a peak and then taper off to static forces once things stop moving. It is critical to understand how peak forces are created, because when slings snap and anchors blow out, it is the consequence of peak forces. This is such a fundamental point that climbing's entire safety system should be viewed in terms of peak force management.

DYNAMIC FORCES IN A FALL

In his outstanding book, *The Mountaineering Handbook,* alpinist and scientist Craig Connally presents a new take on the forces involved in a real world factor 2 fall. His findings, conclusions and words, which are the principal source of this discussion (we collaborated on this chapter), differ substantially from the common understanding extrapolated from lab tests, and for one basic reason: The simulated drop test does not employ the safety system used by actual climbers on actual climbs.

Basically the drop test is an exercise in shock-loading a system that is entirely static save for the 2.8 meters of dynamic climbing rope. In real world climbing, flex and give are present in many components of the safety system, and when that flex and give is accounted for, along with rope slip in the belay device, the force numbers (and the implications of same) are substantially lower than those provided by a UIAA factor 2 drop test.

According to Connally, the lower forces are primarily due to the fact that in a real life factor 2 fall, normal tube or plate belay devices function far differently than the inflexible anchor tie-off in the lab tests. It can be no other way since, Connally says, the maximum force a modern belay device can put on the rope without slipping is 2 or 3 kN. That means the maximum force that any fall can put on the belayer is south of 675 lbf.

In those rare cases where the climber falls directly onto the belay anchor, Connally figures that forces on the climber and belay anchor in a factor 2 fall are relatively low (about 2 to 3 kN), which is only slightly more than a hanging climber could create by thrashing around. He says during a factor 1 fall, rope slip in the belay device would again limit peak force on the belayer to a couple of kN (this time upward rather than downward), and that the force on the climber would be only slightly higher (about 3 kN), due to friction through the top carabiner. However the force on the highest anchor between them (in a simple system) would be the sum of the force on the climber and the force on the belayer. Overall Connally figures that the highest real world force on the top anchor would be in the range of 5.5 to 8.5 kN—roughly 1,900 pounds at the top end, and possibly lower than 1,250 lbf (he talks about things that would increase or decrease these forces). That's much less than the 12 kN maximum that the UIAA allows in the drop test, a test in which the rope is tied off. Of course, in a real world fall, the rope is not tied off. It's belayed, and the belay slips.

Again, during high-factor falls energy absorption at the belay (due to rope slippage) soaks up considerable fall energy, keeping forces lower than those of the lab drop test or even the impact force rating of most ropes. When all energy-absorbing factors are taken into account, it's likely that peak forces on the climber and belayer will be lower still. According to Connally:

> "The previous calculations assumed that the climber is an iron weight tied directly to the rope. A real climber is a flexible object attached to the rope by a conforming harness. Distortion of the falling climber's body will reduce forces about 5 percent, and harness distortion will absorb another 5 percent during typical falls. Lifting of the belayer's body may also reduce peak forces by a significant amount, maybe 10 to as much as 20 percent, if design of the belay permits. The overall consequence is that fall forces for short falls are less than those calculated (in the lab drop test) because of all these various factors that absorb energy and reduce peak forces."

Connally is not alone in believing that the forces suggested by lab drop tests are greater than those sustained in the field. Chris Harmston, Black Diamond's quality assurance manager, reviewed field failures of climbing gear for eight years. He never saw a Stopper rated at over 10 kN fail, and only saw a few carabiners fail in closed-gate mode. He concluded that forces exceeding 10 kN rarely happen in climbing falls.

This is telling because a BD Stopper is among the most commonly used protection device in all trad climbing. It's certain that Stoppers have held countless worst-case scenario falls. They are rated at 10 kN, so if not one has ever failed, it's a sure bet that forces of 10 kN have never been logged on any rock climb. The lack of even a single 10 kN rated stopper failing, in the entire history of the sport, suggests that the 10 kN rating (2,250 lbf) has never been seriously challenged, and that actual forces of factor 2 falls are likely to be less than even Connally's high-end figure of 8.5 kN (roughly 1,900 lbf).

This shows a climber running the lead rope through the anchor points as he takes off on lead. If he should fall, his full weight will come onto the anchor, not the belayer, which is a mixed blessing. It might mean less force directly on the belayer, but it will double the forces on the anchor. Better for this climber to forego running the rope through the anchor and instead place a bomber Jesus Nut as soon as possible, probably from his current stance, where the crack looks willing to accept a good piece.

So far we've heard Connally assert that the belayer sustains less than 3 kN peak force. He goes on to show how the "top piece," be it a component of the belay anchor, the first piece of pro off the belay or the last piece high above, is subject to— at the very most—somewhere around 1,900 lbf. Moreover this calculation is based on the climber being an iron block. Swap out the iron block with a human body, and the forces might drop to as little as 1,520 lbf at the top end. This is far less than the force measured in lab drop tests, where there is no belayer, no belay device and no rope slip, and no give and flex from the climber's body and the rigging typically found in a real world belay anchor. The obvious implication of all this is that the top-most pro is the most impor- tant in the entire roped safety system, since it always sustains the greatest loading (and the leader and belayer might both end up hanging from it).

Conclusion: The main task of the belay is to limit loading on the top-most pro, a process that is highly facilitated by rope slippage in modern belay devices. Further force reduction is provided by the other flex and give in a normal belay setup, not the least of which is the belayer's body, providing a counterweight to cancel out much of the upward force. Clearly a belay and a belay anchor with these characteristics bears little resem- blance to a lab drop test, where an iron weight (the climber) is not belayed at all.

THE TOP PIECE

Even though the forces in a real life factor 2 fall are less than those registered in the lab drop test, we never want to fall directly onto the belay anchor, no matter if the forces are 5 lbf or 5,000 lbf. The whole point of placing protection is for the pro, not the belay anchor, to arrest the fall. That is why we fashion the belay to function as a peak force load limiter to keep loading on the top piece as low as possible. And since we never want to fall directly onto the belay anchor, the most critical time is when we might possibly do so, when the leader is first leaving the belay and has yet to place that first piece of protection. After the first pro is placed, any fall force on the belayer will always be up (not down), potentially reducing the static force (the belayer's weight) on the anchor. Conversely, fall force on the top piece will always be down (and maybe out), and that dynamic force will be considerable.

This leads to a basic safety credo: What deserves our most critical attention is the first placement after the belay anchor, the so-called Jesus Nut (a term that generically applies to any and all protection devices, from pitons to bolts to nuts, etc.).

THE JESUS NUT

"Jesus Nut" is a term made infamous by helicopter mechanics during the Vietnam war. The then-ubiquitous Bell UH-1 "Huey" Iroquois helicopter had one and only one giant, stainless steel nut (the Jesus Nut) that screwed onto the top of the main rotor mast, keeping the main rotor blades attached to the copter. As the saying went, "If it fails, the next person you see will be Jesus."

If a leader falls and the Jesus Nut fails, the belay anchor becomes the last line of defense by default and must be built with that worst-case scenario in mind. Anything less is not good enough. But in real life rock climbing, most any leader fall directly onto the belay anchor is almost always avoidable, and was generally preceded by significant errors in judgment.

For example, a team cannot suffer catastrophic anchor failure unless the leader falls. If you misjudge the caliber of the Jesus Nut, climb on, fall off and the Jesus Nut rips, that's one error in judgment. If you cannot secure a reliable Jesus Nut, carry on anyhow and pitch off, you've either overestimated your ability to climb a section of rock without falling or trusted rock that failed. Finally, if the belay anchor itself fails, it was not "good enough"; you broke the Golden Rule and paid for it with your life.

On established rock climbs, the times that a team encounters a suspect belay anchor, above which a bombproof Jesus Nut is impossible to acquire, on rock too difficult or too loose to climb, and under conditions in which you must try and climb on anyway, are so rare they're hardly worth mentioning. Such dire conditions are infrequently

The Golden Rule

- An anchor system is not good enough unless it can withstand the greatest force that can possibly be put to it, known as a factor 2 fall.

encountered even on new routes, and when they are, the bolt gun usually comes out. Alpine climbers (Connally's targeted audience) regularly confront these circumstances, which might be why so many of them die. If you ever find yourself in such straits, either rap off, or if that's impossible, start yelling for a rescue. If you choose to carry on, understand that you're basically free soloing—and if one goes, you're both goners.

Climbers on the extremely runout *Bachar-Yerian* route in Toulumne. Notice how the first bolt placed by the leader is only a few feet above the belay—this will help absorb the force of a fall rather than having all that force put directly on the anchor. The sooner you can put in that first bomber piece, the better. If you're placing natural gear, an SLCD works well because of its multidirectional capabilities.

CONCLUSION

Effective force management requires that we build a "good enough" belay anchor and set a secure Jesus Nut directly off the belay. This is preventative medicine that essentially backs up the belay anchor. The Jesus Nut is not some auxiliary component we add if convenient, rather it's a crucial element of the belay anchor itself, the redundant element that just might save your ass. Many climbers try to make Jesus, so to speak, an SLCD, which has some multidirectional qualities. People often double up and equalize this first piece, applying the same SRENE principles as those used for the belay anchor. If a leader fall directly onto the belay is even a remote possibility, the anchor must be built to serve as protection (much more on this later) with the understanding that if it fails, "the next person you see will be Jesus." No helicopter pilot in his right mind would take off if there were any chance at all of the Jesus Nut failing. Likewise, no one climbs above an anchor that might be fallen upon and that might fail.

While what you place can take many forms, the importance of the Jesus Nut cannot be overstated. When both the belay anchor and the Jesus Nut check out, the roped safety system is truly on line. If not, it's a gamble, and you're "all in" every time.

WHAT DOES THAT STANDARDS STAMP STAND FOR?

You may see standards abbreviations on ropes and other hardware. The CE mark (Communauté Européenne or Conformité Européenne or just an abstract logo, depending on whom you believe) isn't intended as a mark of quality; instead it indicates that the product's manufacturer claims compliance with applicable directives (Euro-speak for standards). These can include certain requirements for quality and performance and, in the case of "personal protective equipment to protect against falls from a height," safety. Climbing hardware products must have the CE mark to be sold in Europe. The number following the mark indicates the test facility, not the directives or standards that the product claims to meet; so you may find different products with the same number, or similar products with different numbers.

The CEN (Comité Européen de Normalisation or European Committee for Standards) issues EN (European Norm) standards specific to the type of product; these standards may have any number of safety, performance and testing requirements. The EN standard for dynamic climbing ropes, for example, is EN 892. The UIAA standard 101 is comparable. The UIAA mark is sometimes printed inside a little mountain-shaped logo. You may also encounter reference to ISO 9000. This is a paperwork standard that doesn't indicate quality or performance but signifies that the manufacturer's processes, including quality testing, are well documented. It suggests that the manufacturer has its act together overall. You'll increasingly see ISO 14000 certificates, indicating the manufacturer implements and documents an acceptable environmental management policy.

Source: *The Mountaineering Handbook* by Craig Connally. Used with permission.

Climbers on the classic *Ancient Art,* Fisher Towers, Utah. PHOTO BY STEWART M. GREEN.

CHAPTER SIX

Judging the Direction of Pull

Now that we have reviewed the ways in which static and dynamic forces are generated and controlled in climbing, we need to see exactly how those forces are transmitted through the components of the roped safety system. This topic is generally referred to as "direction of pull," meaning that a given force will *pull* on the system from a specific *direction(s)*. No matter how well you understand the nature and the numbers about dynamic and static forces, unless you know where those forces are coming from, your rigging and anchor building will be founded on guesswork, not specific knowledge.

We have previously touched on direction of pull in various places. Now it's time to thoroughly grasp one of the most crucial aspects of the climbing game. At a given belay on a given climb, the direction of pull will influence your choice of two rigging strategies: statically equalized or dynamically equalized—subjects we devote considerable time to exploring in the following chapters. In short, you can't go about rigging an anchor to protect loading angles for which you are unaware. You need to know the direction of pull. Judging the direction of pull is as intuitive as knowing where the sun rises, providing you have a clear mental picture of what the pull is and how it is transmitted through the rope. Understanding the physics involved (forces) taught us the essential qualities of this pull. Now let's look at the picture of those forces at play.

Imagine yourself on a flat, wide-open field while facing due north. You are anchored to a cherry tree directly behind and have the "soft" (belay) end of a 50-foot piece of rope wrapped around your waist. The business end of the rope runs to the waist of your partner who is standing in front of you. Your partner (the leader) walks 30 feet due north to an orange tree, then walks just past the tree and begins running due west (directly left). After 20 more feet, the leader runs out of rope. His forward momentum is stopped by the rope, transmitting a pull *through* the rope that runs back to you. Even though the leader has traversed 20 feet off due north, the direction of pull on the anchor is still due north, where the rope runs around the orange tree. That is, the direction of pull does not come from where the leader is once the rope comes tight—20 feet dead left of the orange tree—rather it comes from the orange tree because A) the "pull" is transmitted *through* the rope, and B) the rope runs *around* the orange tree.

The exact same dynamic occurs on a leader fall. *The direction of pull is described by a direct line between you (the belay) and the first piece of protection through which the rope runs.* When belaying someone following a pitch, the direction pull is described by the last piece of pro through which the rope runs.

Obviously to properly judge the direction of pull, you need to know where the route goes. In our first example, when you were standing in the middle of a flat field, you could see the orange tree due north, so the direction of pull was obvious. But unless you're heading for a bolt or other fixed protection, it's hard to know exactly where the leader will place the first piece of pro—the Jesus Nut—and you won't know till Jesus is in place. And until Jesus is placed and clipped off, you can't know the exact direction of pull. But by observing the rock above the belay, and by referencing the topo (if you have one), you can normally predict the direction of the next lead—perhaps not exactly, but usually within 5 or so degrees.

Climbs following prominent cracks and chimneys clearly follow an obvious and certain direction, and the protection, and the direction of pull, can be extrapolated from the line of the obvious crack. But move out of conspicuous crack systems and the direction of pull can become less clear, particularly on face routes that wander around blind corners or connect various features on an open face. While no climb can go every direction at once, a leader might wander extravagantly trying to find the easiest route, placing protection first on the left and then on the right. This means the direction of pull can also change.

On vertical crack systems, the direction of pull is either straight down, in the case of a second climbing up to the belayer, or straight up, when the leader leaves the belay on the next pitch and clips the lead rope through protection placed in the vertical crack. In most every other case, the direction of pull will be in a direct line between the anchor and the pro nearest the anchor, in whatever direction that may be.

To clarify, if you're belaying someone seconding (following) a pitch and the protection nearest the belay is a nut 10 feet down and 3 feet left of the fall line, if the second should fall before reaching the belay, the rope will snap taut between you (the anchor) and the nut down and left. If you're belaying a leader who has traversed straight left off the belay and clipped a bolt 10 feet out left, if the leader falls, the direction of pull will be directly out and left, so long as the protection holds.

When you're belaying someone following a pitch, the direction of pull is obvious because in the event of a fall, the rope will always come tight (consider the rope as an arrow pointing to the direction of pull) in a direct line between you and the last piece of gear. And you know where that last piece is because you placed it or you clipped it. But as mentioned, when leading, unless you're heading for conspicuous fixed gear, who can say where the first protection will be placed; therefore you can't exactly predict where the direction of pull will come from. But normally the general direction is at least somewhat clear.

DIRECTION OF PULL AND ANCHOR BUILDING

Determining the direction of pull is crucial because a belay anchor is often built to safeguard against specific directions of pull, and not against directions of pull that cannot occur on a given pitch. Anchors that protect against specific directions of pull are called "statically equalized" (aka pre-equalized) anchors. Anchors that protect against multiple directions of pull are called "dynamically equalized" (aka self-

The climber following this pitch is unclipping the last piece. As long as that piece is still clipped, the direction of pull on the belayer and anchor in the event of a fall will be in a straight line toward that last piece. However, when the piece is unclipped, the direction of pull will be in an arc below the belayer, and the anchor better be built to withstand the swinging load. It's no problem with this bolted belay, but hand-built anchors require careful thought. PHOTO BY STEWART M. GREEN.

DIRECTION OF PULL

■ Every fall generates a dynamic force that will *pull* on the roped safety system from a specific *direction or directions*.

■ The direction of pull is described by a direct line between the belayer and the first piece (when belaying a leader) of pro, or the last piece of pro (when belaying a follower) through which the rope runs.

■ Lead protection and belay anchors must sustain loading from every direction of pull that is possible on a specific pitch.

■ To accurately judge the direction of pull, you must know where the route goes.

■ When the direction of pull is uncertain, a multidirectional belay anchor is required.

■ When a swinging fall directly onto protection, or onto the belay anchor, is possible, the pro and the belay anchor must be built to sustain loading across the full arc of the swing.

■ Knowing the direction of pull is to a climber what knowing the direction of a possible ambush is to a foot soldier: *essential for survival.*

equalizing) anchors, subjects that by the end of this book will be ground into your very bone marrow.

It should be pointed out that, barring routes with a lot of traversing, some climbers don't much factor the direction of pull into their anchors, especially when the primary placements are bomber and the route follows a relatively plumb line trajectory. Here the anchor consists of bomber pro (especially the Jesus Nut), a good stance and the rope—enough for some climbers to feel confident they can handle all loads in all likely directions of pull (mainly straight up and down). While optimum equalization might be absent in such anchors, between stout primary placements, rope stretch, flex and give in the rigging system—and using the body as counterweight against loading from whatever direction it might come—many climbers feel comfortable the anchor is good enough.

This practice leads to a question commonly asked: If we understand the directions of pull, why build an anchor to safeguard against direction(s) of pull that can never occur on a given climb? Isn't that a little like facing a solar panel away from the sun, or building a guest house for friends who will never visit? Well, not exactly.

If we always climbed on bolted sport routes or in laser-cut vertical cracks, there would be little reason to ever build belays with a wide-loading axis, resulting in a multidirectional anchor. We could simply design the belay to target the anticipated directions of pull—with a few degrees to spare—and we'd be mint.

In actual practice many climbers assess the direction of pull and build the anchor so it can withstand a worst-case scenario fall only in that direction or directions. Why safeguard against sideways forces, say, when the route goes straight up and down? Moreover, some argue, convincingly at times, the need for placements to sustain upward loading is also unnecessary, a discussion we'll engage in shortly. There are pros and cons for each argument, but several recent anchor failures bring another, seldom-mentioned factor into the equation. Namely, swing.

SWING

Consider our previous example, when the leader traverses straight left off the belay, places a piece and falls. What happens when the piece rips out? The leader's fall will describe a 90-degree arc, and then some, and the direction of pull will come from various rapidly changing vectors in a phenomenon called swing.

With swing, gravity is forcing, at a rapidly accelerating rate, a climber's falling body directly into the fall line, which is always a direct line below the last piece through which the rope is clipped, or directly onto the anchor if a Jesus Nut has not been arranged or blows out in a fall. This swing is simply a pendulum coming to rest. When the leader swings onto the anchor as described, he will not load the system in the standard, quick-loading fashion. The loading during the first few feet of straight-down fall is not much, but the forces rapidly increase as the falling climber begins to weight the rope and arc toward the fall line. While there is little lab information detailing the fine points of swing-loading on an anchor, common sense tells us that the anchor best be sufficiently multidirectional to sustain loading across the entire 90-degree arc of the falling climber's swing—and a little beyond as well—since the anchor will likely sustain lesser to greater loading throughout the entire arc.

The above must be kept in mind when the leader is just climbing off the belay and when there's a possibility that the Jesus Nut might fail—always a very dangerous proposition. If a leader falls before arranging the Jesus Nut, or if the Jesus Nut blows, the leader will fall past the belay twice the distance he is out from the belay when he fell. The extent that the leader has climbed left or right of the anchor is the range of swing vectors that will be placed on the anchor. The greatest loading will likely occur when the falling leader's vertical path comes tight and is converted to a roughly circular arc, thereby forcing the anchor to sustain an "off-axis" impact. After this point the leader's full weight will be on the rope as he swings into the fall line and beyond. Several recent anchor failures suggest that swinging forces put significant and screwy forces on anchors. In short, if the anchors have not been built with those forces in mind, and these forces occur, people can and do perish.

Case in point was a recent fatal anchor failure at the top of Tahquitz Rock, in Southern California. While we cannot be certain of anything, the components of the failed anchor—which remained attached to the rope after the accident—gave strong evidence suggesting that the leader had placed an anchor in a horizontal crack near,

This leader has traversed left off the belay, and if she falls before clipping that first piece (the Jesus Nut), the load on the anchor will describe an approximately 90-degree arc below the belayer. If the anchor is built to withstand only a straight up or down pull, this could spell trouble. (Barefoot belaying, although comfy, is not recommended!) PHOTO BY STEWART M. GREEN.

or at the top, of the rock. When the second followed the pitch, he fell at a point when he was not in the fall line, meaning he was a ways left or right of the anchor overhead. The fall apparently put a swing load onto the anchor, which ripped out and sent the two climbers to their deaths. (The anchors were likely placed in poor quality rock, which possibly contributed to this anchor failure. How much—we can never know.)

This tragedy illustrates that even when belaying someone following a pitch, where the fall factors are far less than for lead falls, swinging loads can wreck havoc with anchors. Again, the changing and accelerating loading vectors of a swinging fall likely wrench the anchors in ways and in directions that potentially spell doom for any anchor not specifically designed to sustain them (i.e., multidirectional).

Bottom line: When a swinging fall is possible, any anchor that is not fashioned to withstand loading across the full arc of the swing and a few degrees beyond is not good enough.

While there are arguments against rigging multidirectional, dynamically equalized anchors in some cases—specifically when the direction of pull is known and remains a constant—such anchors are essential whenever a swinging fall is even remotely possible. Remember that so long as the first piece of protection above the belay holds (in the event of a leader fall), no matter where the leader climbs after that first piece, and no matter where she places protection past that first piece, the direction of pull will remain directly in line with that first piece. It can work no other way, since the force is transmitted *through* the rope, and the rope runs *through* the first pro.

Understanding the direction of pull is as important to a climber as understanding the direction of an ambush is to a foot soldier. Both are wise to keep an eye in *all* directions, but especially toward the direction of obvious threat—and for a climber building an anchor, the greatest threat comes precisely from the direction of pull. Whenever an old guide sees a belayer not in line with the direction of pull, the standard joke is to ask the student if he puts the seat belt on behind him when he drives a car because he obviously doesn't understand the direction of pull.

DIRECTION OF PULL ON PRIMARY PLACEMENTS

As mentioned, with secure pitons, bolts and trees (to list a few multidirectional anchors), you can yank from any direction and the anchor is good. Nuts and cams work on an entirely different principle and are secure only within a limited range of loading. Equalization techniques, though never perfect, allow us to greatly increase the direction(s) an anchor can be impacted while at the same time distributing the impact force over the components of the anchor matrix. In theory we'd like to enjoy 360 degrees of equal security, meaning we could pull on the anchor from any direction along the plane of the rock, and the load on the anchor would never change. This is a true, omnidirectional anchor. Unfortunately it's unlikely we can ever perfectly achieve this, nor do we have to.

For example, consider the common scenario where you're left to fashion an anchor in one or more closely aligned vertical cracks. Typically, in good rock with ready placements, you will slot several bomber nuts for a downward pull, then rig these against several lower nuts rigged for an upward pull. Even with textbook rigging, most every anchor can best sustain up and down forces. In other words, the anchor is stronger if you pulled up on it, or directly down on it, as opposed to pulling directly on it from the left or right side. A direct up or down force pulls directly in the attitude for which the nuts were designed to absorb loading, and in which they were placed. You're rigging might be so expertly arranged that the load is shared fairly equally by the primary placements, but the primary placements themselves are strongest when pulled in limited, not unlimited, directions.

Sage rigging can compensate for oblique forces on hand-placed gear, but never to the extent that sideways vectors will place exactly the same force when the nuts were impacted in their optimum orientation. Nor will the best rigging always and entirely eliminate the primary placements being loaded in directions in which the placements are not especially robust. The only way for this to be possible is if you perfectly equalized (impossible) primary placements that were themselves omnidirectional, such as bolts and pitons. Many cam placements can pivot somewhat within the crack and still remain sound. Passive nuts such as tapers are generally reliable only when loaded in one direction, though bottleneck placements increase that range. The process of rigging a combination of these components into an effective anchor matrix will be discussed shortly, after we go over a few necessary knots.

Dennis Jump belays Martha Morris on Hitchcock Pinnacle, Mount Lemmon, Arizona. PHOTO BY STEWART M. GREEN.

CHAPTER SEVEN

Knots for Anchoring

Knots play an essential role in creating anchor systems and tying into them. A handful of knots will cover the job nicely, so there's no need to get into trick or show knots. Know that Jim Bridwell, one of the most experienced climbers in the history of the sport, uses only four knots for any and all climbing situations. Better to learn a few knots well, than a multitude of knots poorly.

RING BEND

Also known as the water knot, the ring bend is used to tie sections of webbing into slings. Check the ring bend every time you use the sling to make sure the tails are at least 3 inches long and the knot is cinched tight. The water knot has a penchant for creeping and untying itself if not properly tightened.

DOUBLE FISHERMAN'S

The double fisherman's, or fisherman's knot, is a much more secure but bulky knot for tying slings together. The double fisherman's knot is also used to tie two rappel ropes together. For high-tensile cord, the triple fisherman's is recommended. A double fisherman's in webbing creeps much more slowly than a ring bend, but still it should be checked periodically to make sure the tails are sufficiently long.

OVERHAND ON A BIGHT AND FIGURE EIGHT ON A BIGHT

Once you have arranged a belay anchor, you must tie into it. Since you are already tied into the end of the rope, you must use a knot for the middle of the rope—a "loop knot." For this purpose, two knots, the overhand on a bight and the figure eight on a bight, provide the strength and ease of tying that make their use exclusive for the main tie-in to the anchor—the power point. The overhand on a bight is

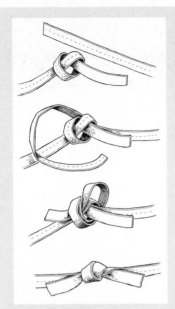

The ring bend (water knot).

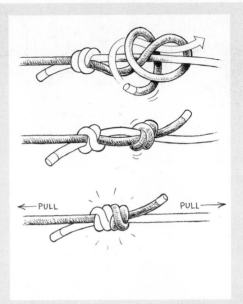

Double fisherman's knot. Add one more loop around each end to make a triple fisherman's knot.

Overhand on a bight.

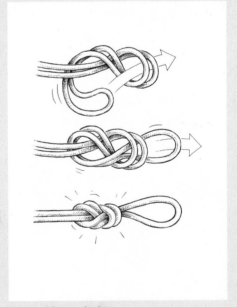

Figure eight on a bight.

the simplest knot imaginable, but once weighted can be a bearcat to untie. The figure eight on a bight is usually better—strong and easy to untie once weighted or shock-loaded. Some climbers initially clip off with a clove hitch, the advantage being the ease of getting things perfectly adjusted. Though a properly tied clove hitch will work fine here, to me the clove looks weird as my one and only tie-in knot, so for purely psychological reasons, I, and many others, go with the figure eight.

CLOVE HITCH

A tie-in knot that is quick and easy to tie, easy to adjust for length once tied, and that unties easily is naturally a knot welcomed by climbers. The clove hitch is such a knot. Some climbers believe the trade-off for all this utility is that clove hitches reportedly slip at around 1,000 pounds of load, although tests have shown that a clove hitch will in fact not slip in a dynamic rope (it can, however, slip in a static rope, making the knot a poor choice for hauling gear or jugging lines). Clove hitches can also work themselves loose. Be sure they are kept tight at the bottom of the carabiner, away from the gate, with the load-bearing strand on the spine side of the biner. The reliability of a clove hitch can be improved by using a pear-shaped locking carabiner.

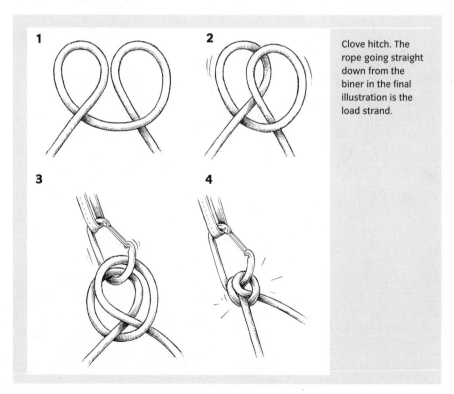

Clove hitch. The rope going straight down from the biner in the final illustration is the load strand.

A clove hitch can be used to tie off oppositional nuts at an anchor.

An esoteric point here about clove hitches: The load-bearing strand of the rope coming from the clove hitch should be aligned near the spine of the carabiner and away from the gate, or you sacrifice nearly one-third of the carabiner's strength should the gate come open. Traditional wisdom says that an anchor should not be arranged exclusively with clove hitches, that the wise climber uses a figure eight somewhere in the anchor system. But I suspect that the "traditional wisdom" reflects what I mentioned earlier about the look of the clove, not its performance. Many climbers feel that the best use of the clove hitch at the belay is to use it as the power point (with a locking biner for adjustability), then back it up with an overhand on a bight or figure eight on a bight to a bomber piece in the anchor system.

That much said, the clove hitch can be a little tricky, and every rookie needs to experiment with a short piece of rope/sling and a biner to get the clove hitch "wired." Because you can easily tie the clove incorrectly, it's essential to know how to properly tie it before doing so in the field. Half an hour of fiddling and the clove is yours for life.

BOWLINE-ON-A-BIGHT

The bowline-on-a-bight has been around since Noah's Ark and has long been a favorite in rescue work, but only recently has it been espoused as an alternative knot, almost always for rigging static rope for toprope anchors. Though this knot will never become popular as an anchor-rigging knot, it does have certain applications, and since you might one day see it used in the field, it can't hurt to know how to use it.

The bowline-on-a-bight can be rigged to function much the same as a cordelette, the difference being that the bowline-on-a-bight has only two branches. The b-on-a-bight, as it is sometimes called, can be used to equalize two bolts at a hanging belay. However it's fast to arrange only if you're practiced in its use; otherwise it can take hours. The bowline-on-a-bight can also be used to equalize two points of a multicomponent gear anchor, although other systems presented later in this book are superior.

Much like the clove hitch, the bowline-on-a-bight requires practice to master. The challenge is not learning to tie the knot, but in arranging the two double

How to tie a bowline-on-a-bight.

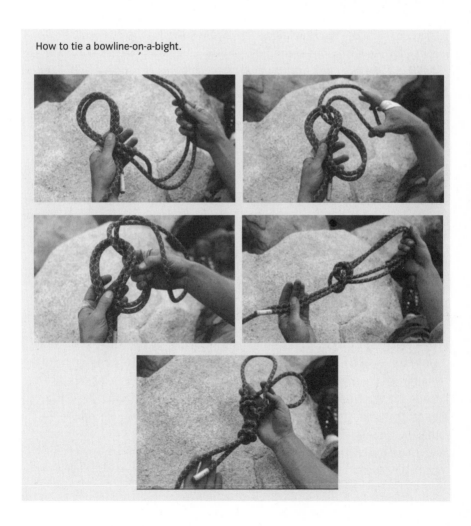

TWO BINERS AT THE POWER POINT

Though we will dive into this later, and in greater depth, whatever knots you use, I recommend to never arrange the power point with only one carabiner. Yes, this has become common practice with AMGA guides: clove hitch to one locking biner. But for my money, such a nonredundant method relies too heavily on a single piece of gear that can easily hide flaws—and the gate might get torqued open by a bight of rope. A slim chance, granted, but you don't want to take any chances, so use two carabiners, gates opposed, or better yet, a locking carabiner and a regular back-up carabiner.

strands at appropriate lengths to clip off at two varying points. Consider this: If two bolts are positioned one above the other, the two double strands of the knot must be of different lengths to accomplish equalization. This is achieved by tying the knot loosely, clipping the double strands into the two anchor points, then snugging the knot up accordingly. This sounds more involved than it is, but if you don't thoroughly learn the knot, it's deceivingly tricky to rig well and efficiently. Again, while the bowline-on-a-bight is a viable knot, it will never catch on as a primary rigging knot.

MUNTER HITCH

Popular legend insists the Munter hitch was first used by stevedores to tether onerous loads on the waterfront. Later a German purportedly took the concept, applied it to climbing and named the method after his own self. The French company, Petzl, calls the Munter the "Italian Munter Hitch," insisting that an Italian with a German name brought the technique to Paris. Perhaps Munter is a Swede living in Senegal and has never heard of any hitch. It remains a mystery. . . .

Regardless, when climbers transitioned from hip belays to the now-standard friction belay devices, the Munter hitch was frequently employed. Nowadays the Munter hitch is used on long routes to save weight, or when you're so unfortunate to have dropped your belay device. Since this does happen, and might happen to you, you either learn the Munter hitch and go with that, or revert to the hip belay.

When using the Munter hitch, always align the load-bearing strand (going to the climber) with the spine side, not the gate side, of the locking biner. As with all hitches, the Munter hitch will kink the rope unless it is allowed to run loosely through the biner. This does not mean there should be much slack in the hitch, rather that you should avoid pulling the slack in with the brake hand, which naturally crimps the hitch on itself and on the biner. For a toproped climber, feed the rope to the Munter hitch, doing 80 percent of the work with your guide hand as the

The Munter hitch.

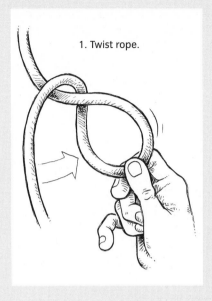

1. Twist rope.

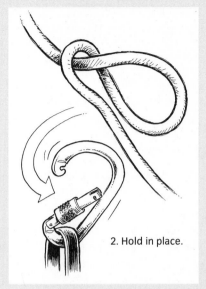

2. Hold in place.

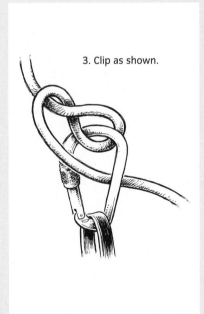

3. Clip as shown.

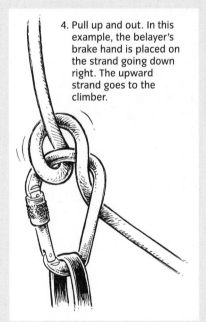

4. Pull up and out. In this example, the belayer's brake hand is placed on the strand going down right. The upward strand goes to the climber.

brake hand gently pulls in the slack (never pulling hard enough for the hitch to bind). When belaying a leader, the guide hand gently pulls the rope out above the hitch. The function of this pulling and feeding on both sides is to ensure easy action by eliminating the direct weight and friction of the climbing rope on the hitch. When there's no weight on the hitch, it runs smoothly.

Like many techniques, getting fluent with Munter—be he Italian, German or other—takes some practice. Secure toprope settings are ideal to learn this technique. If you wait for an emergency to learn how to get jiggy with the Munter hitch, you've waited too long.

KNOT STRENGTH

For many years there has been talk about knot strength, though there is precious little proof that knot strength is a factor in the field. The few knots we use in climbing all have limitations, but in terms of knots tied into the lead rope, strength is rarely, if ever, one of them. Lab tests prove that knots generally weaken the material with which they are tied. But the materials used in a climbing rope have to my knowledge never failed because a clove hitch, an overhand or a figure eight compromised the strength of the rope so much that the material simply broke solely because of the knot. Providing the rope is in working order, there is so much overkill built into rope that the strength differentials between the few knots we use are a moot point.

On the other hand, some knots tied into high-tensile cord greatly reduce the overall strength of the cordage and should never be used. Independent tests show that high-tensile cord, when tied into a loop with a figure eight on a bight, lost about 40 percent of its strength at the knot. With a tensile breaking strength of around 5,000 pounds for 5.5mm high-tensile cord, this still would hold a good 3,000 pounds. But why use a material in the weakest possible way?

Simply tie all high-tensile cord with a triple fisherman's knot and leave it tied that way for miscellaneous uses, which guarantees no significant loss of strength in the material.

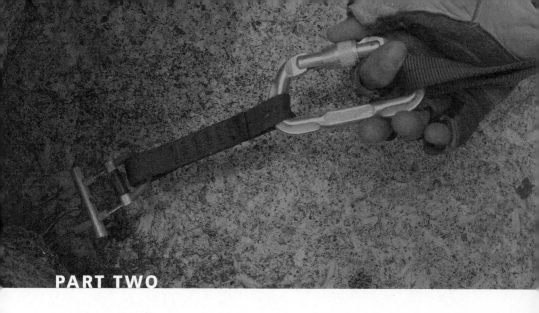

PART TWO

ANCHOR SYSTEMS

Complex anchors consist of multiple primary placements, connected together to provide redundant and multidirectional belay anchors, toprope anchors, rappel anchors and bivouac anchors.

If no substantial natural anchor—a tree, block or large bush—is available on your chosen climb, you must construct an artificial anchor using hand-placed gear. Given that you understand how to place nuts and cams, the trick becomes how to connect them together to create a viable anchor system. Constructing a multipiece anchor will at first take time and trouble, but a trained eye, the knack for finding propitious nut slots and experience with the various rigging methods usually make this routine after a short while. On most trad routes climbers are called to build multinut anchors many times each outing, so the training comes quickly.

If you learn one thing from this book, let it be the **Golden Rule:** An anchor system is not good enough unless it can withstand the greatest force that can possibly be put to it, known as a factor 2 fall. This is common sense, plain and simple. The fact that there are comparatively few instances of outright belay, toprope or rappel anchor failures suggests that climbers are particularly observant of the Golden Rule. However it could also suggest that the Golden Rule is very rarely put

Climbers on the wildly exposed route *The Shield,* El Capitan, California. PHOTO BY BOB GAINES.

to the test, and when anchors do fail, tragedy usually follows. Every climber should occasionally thumb through any number of annual journals about accidents in climbing. Here you'll see that few survive a total anchor failure—all the more reason to bear with the discussion, long and entangled as it may be.

Before we get into specifics, let's review some general concepts concerning what not to do. First, never belay from one anchor point unless it's a tree the size of the Washington Monument, or a block bigger than the Sphinx. Even so, redundancy is security. However if you climb long enough, you're bound to run into a situation where you have to belay from a single anchor—perhaps a poor one. Allow me an anecdote here to show you just how dreadful it can be.

The Shield is neither the grimmest nor the longest aid route on El Capitan, but toward the top of that vast, overhanging curtain of orange granite, the exposure is strictly world class. At the end of one of those long knifeblade pitches, I hit a rivet ladder and finally the belay—a hanging one, of course, from one sorry, rusted, mushroomed, buttonhead bolt. Without a hanger. This was in the mid-seventies, before the route had seen many ascents and obviously before anyone had bolstered the anchors. Anyway, the haulbag, Mike Lechlinski and I found ourselves hanging on that single, miserable bolt. The rivet ladder above looked bleak, more so because the previous ascent party had tied off every rivet with hero loops that had somehow cinched so tight we couldn't get them off without a knife, which, of course, we didn't have. This ascent had taken place the previous summer, and over the winter the hero loops had bleached and frayed, and currently flapped in the wind like little threads of gauze.

As Mike took off, holding his breath on every frazzled loop, on every creaking rivet, I tried to study the river below, or watch cars creep along the loop road, 2,500 feet down. But every few seconds my eyes would snap back to that sorry bolt. I saw it rotate in the hole. I heard it creak, then snap like a toothpick. Twice I saw it melt out of the hole. I put my thumb over it, both thumbs over it. I imagined a loop snapping on one of those rivets, and Mike zippering down onto that jive bolt, which surely would pop, and I wept pitifully and pissed my pants. I made a quick and binding pact with our Savior that if I ever got off that stinking rock alive, I'd devote my life to the poor and bereft. It was a horrible experience.

Next consideration: Never trust a fixed anchor setup outright, no matter how bombproof it appears. Many things can disguise just how poor an anchor may be, particularly a huge knot of slings from previous parties who obviously trusted the thing. Why shouldn't you? Consider the big stump that used to be atop Arch Rock in Yosemite. There were no less than fifty runners slung around it; thousands of climbers had belayed and rappelled off it for twenty years. Richard Harrison took the time to check it one day and found that it was loose. We got behind it and pushed with our legs, and the thing popped from the dirt like a mushroom and pitched off the cliff, nearly killing a team of Korean climbers below. It was ready to go, and had been for God knows how long.

The point is, fifty slings don't prove that an anchor isn't garbage. Don't be deceived by an anchor that appears sound, regardless of the fact that other climbers have long trusted it. I could go on and on about what to look for with fixed anchors, but the bottom line will always hinge on two points: Are the component, primary anchor points (be they bolts, fixed pins, nuts or a mix) sound, and if so, are they rigged together in a way that is likewise not only sound, but predicts the direction of possible loading? Examine the anchor and understand why it is good (or bad) before you trust it.

When no fixed anchors exist, you must set your own. In doing so understand that this book is based on several basic principles, none more important than this: The foundation of every anchor is the absolute holding strength of the individual or primary placements. No amount of crafty rigging can compensate for poor primary placements. Know from the start that other authors have other ideas about anchoring priorities. Some contend that component strength is overrated, and that the rigging, the means by which the primary placements are connected, is a more crucial concern in terms of force management throughout the entire safety system—and in fact, force management is really the name of the game. But when you start with bombproof primary anchors, keeping force management in mind, you are better off still. Furthermore the functioning of primary placements are simpler and better understood than the far more complicated and less understood mechanics involved once the primary placements are connected into a multiplacement system. In other words, primary placements are more predictable and easier to control than the system as a whole, so we make damn sure we get all we can out of the primary placements, then proceed from there.

Lastly, over the years I've been involved in analyzing a handful of total anchor failures (all fatal). The process requires investigating the gear that was found on the belayer's rope and reverse-engineering the setup to try and determine the particulars of the failed anchor. In more than a few cases it seemed pretty obvious that textbook rigging had been employed, and that small-to-medium-sized nuts and camming devices had blown out under loading. The fact that other rigging methods might have saved these climbers was a secondary issue for one irrefutable reason: In the same area in which the anchor had failed were options for other primary placements, often bombproof natural anchors such as large blocks or trees, anchors so strong that even with the most rudimentary rigging technique they would have held a cement truck. For these reasons, our system begins with the most fundamental task: **arranging strong primary placements.**

Beyond this basic tenet, keep the following details in mind whenever building anchors:

- Find a spot that provides convenient anchor placements and provides a suitable position for the climber once the anchor is set. Because a falling climber impacts a belayer's body at the belay device, and because the give of a belayer serves as a crucial load-reduction element in the belay chain, an anchor will ideally be located a few feet directly above the belayer. What you want in a belay system is one that will limit peak loading through the collective give and flex in the system. The dynamic qualities (give and flex) in the belayer's body, the rope slipping through the belay device, the stretch in the slings and, first and foremost, the elasticity in the lead rope, all serve to gently slow down the accelerating mass, as opposed to stopping it all at once, like a head-on collision. While a steel rope and steel slings would be stronger than stretchy nylon, they would provide no dynamic decelerating give or stretch and would arrest a plummeting load so abruptly and with such an intense shock load that biners would break and cams would blow apart. Without the dynamic qualities in the belay system, it simply would not work.

- After selecting a location and securing yourself to that first placement, take a moment to plan the entire system. Analyze the situation and fashion the anchors to withstand loading from all possible directions of pull.

- Keep the system as simple as possible, so it is quick to set and easy to double-check and monitor. Use the minimal amount of gear to safely and efficiently do the job, which is usually three or four bombproof anchors, and more if they are less than bombproof.

- Remember that the placements are only as strong as the rock they are set in.

- Strive to make anchors SRENE: Solid, Redundant, Equalized, and allowing No Extension, so far as you can. See the next chapter for a discussion of SRENE.

CHAPTER EIGHT

SRENE Anchors

SRENE is an acronym for Solid, Redundant, Equalized, and No Extension first connived by professional guide Marc Chauvin, for use when teaching clients anchoring fundamentals. Marc's first acronym was RENE. S (Solid) was later added, resulting in SRENE, which was appropriated by the IFMGA (International Federation of Mountain Guides Association), and later by me in the first anchor book.

Since its inception SRENE has for many climbers become a sort of fixed-in-stone checklist to which every anchor must conform. This is not only a perversion of the original intention of SRENE, it is physically impossible when SRENE qualities are sought in absolute literal terms. But that hasn't kept people from trying, which over the last decade has spawned a breaking wave of commentary based on everything from Newtonian physics to blue wind. Those favoring this or that aspect of SRENE have squared off like Sumo wrestlers, charging each other with the passion of True Defenders of the Faith. But like everyone married to doctrine, they find themselves yarding on crumbly holds because when considered as inflexible doctrine, SRENE embraces mutually exclusive qualities. For instance, with hand-placed gear you can rarely if ever achieve simultaneous non-extension and equalization. And in the real world, redundancy is not always possible—though always desirable. Mountaineer and engineer Craig Connally, in *The Mountaineering Handbook*, puts it this way: "If static equalization invariably boils down to redundancy rather than true equalization, and dynamic equalization doesn't lead to true shock loading, the old acronyms [SRENE] leave us adrift. What then is a reasonable, realistic approach to building anchors?"

The only "reasonable and realistic" approach to building anchors is to leave off considering SRENE as an absolute doctrine or checklist, and to use SRENE for the purpose for which it was originally devised: as an anchor evaluation methodology. If you were to make a list of traits you'd like in a mate, and settled for nothing less

Keith McAllister on *Tongulation,* New River Gorge, West Virginia. PHOTO BY STEWART M. GREEN.

than someone who perfectly embodied those traits, you'd remain single for as long as you lived. Same goes for building anchors according to SRENE. Most every anchor is a trade-off according to what is actually required, and because every aspect of SRENE is rarely necessary in any anchor—and you're not going to perfectly achieve them all in any event—SRENE is useful only as an evaluation technology. And to that end, SRENE is the best thing going.

All this might sound overly technical and complicated, but in fact all of these concepts are based on common sense and elementary mechanical laws that are usually self-evident once you gain experience. Still, let us look closer at the fundamental concepts behind SRENE. Kindly settle in for the duration.

Solid means just that. The individual, primary anchors and the system as a whole must be bombproof, able to stop a rogue elephant, without question.

Redundant generally means placing three or four solid anchors (more if the anchors are less than ideal). Never use only one nut. Never. Most experienced climbers don't consider an anchor secure until they have set a minimum of three secure primary placements. Two bombproof anchors is the absolute minimum, and only is acceptable when more are not to be had. In emergencies climbers occasionally will use a single bolt, tree or tied-off boulder for an anchor, but secure backup anchors will greatly reduce the chance of a catastrophe. Likewise, because SRENE is an evaluation technology covering the anchor as a system, elements within the system (biners, slings, etc.) should be backed up. Redundancy also can include setting anchors in more than one crack system, to avoid relying on a single rock feature.

Equalized refers to distributing, as equally as possible, any potential loading to the various primary anchors in the system. The aim is to increase the overall strength of the system and to reduce the chance of a single anchor pulling out under loading. Perfect equalization, or even nearly perfect equalization, is something never fully achieved. A reasonably *distributed* load is more often than not all we actually need. This concept will be revisited in the next chapter during our discussion of rigging methods such as the sliding X and cordelette.

No Extension means that if one of the anchors in the system should fail, the system will not suddenly become slack and drop the climber a short distance, loading the remaining anchors. Recent studies suggest that short extensions in loading are not nearly as severe or dangerous as first thought. Like equalization, this is a concept best covered in our discussion of rigging methods in the next chapter.

While SRENE is what we try to achieve, whenever humanly possible, when building anchors, **simplicity** and **efficiency** are the bywords of how we go about our task.

Simplicity means we strive to keep the anchor basic and streamlined, exploiting the obvious features with the simplest, most obvious primary placements, and using elementary, as opposed to garish, rigging techniques whenever possible. We don't

SRENE Anchors

- Solid
- Redundant
- Equalized
- No Extension

want the anchor equivalent of the Taj Mahal. We want Fort Knox. As we all know, it is usually easier to judge the value of a simple system as opposed to a complicated one, and with every anchor, we're wagering our lives on our judgment that the anchor is "good enough." Keep it simple and live to a great age.

Efficiency means we aim to fashion anchors that are swift to build and easy to clean. To do so we need to be organized and effective in our use of time and equipment. Always searching for the quickest and simplest method, we decide on a strategy and apply it to achieve one basic goal—to build anchors that are "good enough." On long trad routes, we arrive at belays at the end of a lead, when we have the least amount of gear with which to build an anchor, so the need for us to work efficiently cannot be overstated. Sure, we all have an ideal anchor we are striving to build, but more times than not we're left to deal with what we've got, and what we've got is seldom ideal.

SRENE VARIATIONS

Several versions of the SRENE acronym have surfaced over the last decade, including SERENE, ERNEST, NERDSS, DORK, SKUNK, SANE and several others. Each acronym contains the same basic principles (which are typically renamed to fit the acronym), with some mixing what we build (SRENE) with how we build it (simply and efficiently). There's nothing wrong with these acronyms, but there does remain a community-wide need to standardize this basic evaluation technology in the same sense that there is a need to have one name, not ten names, for piton. It is neither simple nor efficient to keep cooking up different acronyms to package the self-same principles. So SRENE it is.

REDUNDANCY: THE ONGOING DISCUSSION

Redundancy, as a valuable quality in anchors, became widely standardized shortly after the first edition of *Climbing Anchors*. Since then the subject has drawn a hailstorm of arguments and counter-arguments about A) what redundancy actually is, and B) the relationship of redundancy and security. Some argue that redundancy and security are synonymous, that one is impossible without the other. This is passionately denied by others, though no one questions the overall importance of redundancy. Since you'll encounter this subject time and again, both in print and in the field, let's review the basic debate.

All anchors consist of various links of primary placements and rigging, and the strength and security of those links will always vary within one anchor matrix. To counter this, we bolster the multiple links within the anchor system through redundancy. Basically, redundancy demands that anchor systems be constructed of multiple components—from the primary placements, to the slings and biners we use in rigging the placements together—so that if any one component fails, the anchor will not fail. In other words a redundant anchor never stakes our life on one piece of gear. Yet in several instances we do just that. We (almost always) climb on one rope, tied into one harness, with one belay/rappel loop, on which—when needed—we use one locking biner connected to one belay device.

This hurls us onto a slippery slope. We can't trot out redundancy as an inviolate rule, and break it at the same time. The question becomes this: Can security only be achieved through redundancy? If so, why do we climb on one rope, one harness, etc. If not, where does this leave us in terms of anchors?

Simply put, a fail-safe anchor, not redundancy per se, is the ultimate goal, and redundancy is only one important tool to achieve that goal. Stated differently, we build fail-safe anchors not to ply a rule (redundancy), but so we don't die. If redundancy helps us build fail-safe anchors, as it almost always does, then we use it whenever possible. But experience will eventually show us that a viable anchor can be achieved, however rarely, without letter-perfect redundancy. Furthermore, in the real world there are places where even the most experienced climbers cannot make redundant every facet of the system, and to claim and insist that you can, and must, is false and misleading.

CLIFF NOTES ON REDUNDANCY

- Redundancy Credo: *Never trust a single piece of gear.*

- Proper redundancy ensures that if any one component fails, the anchor will not automatically fail.

- Redundancy asks that anchor systems be constructed of multiple components—from the primary placements, to the slings and biners used for connecting placements.

- According to NASA, *doubling-up (making redundant) components within any system greatly increases their reliability* (over single component setups). Tripling slightly increases reliability over doubled setups. Quadrupling makes practically no difference.

- In real world climbing you sometimes cannot make redundant every facet of the system, but there is every reason to try.

- A fail-safe anchor, not redundancy per se, is the ultimate goal, and redundancy is only one important tool to achieve that goal.

In studying ideal ways to build anchors, here and in a hundred other sources, climbers are sometimes led to believe the rock will always accommodate a textbook setup. It won't, a fact that an overwhelming number of readers demanded I point out. Every experienced climber has on occasion wandered off-route and onto terrain where they were forced to arrange anchors with no redundancy whatsoever. It would be a betrayal to imply this can never happen, that all of your anchors can be perfect.

Nevertheless, piss-poor anchors are for most climbers an infrequent experience. By and large there are adequate anchors to be had, and when there are, it all boils down to this: On the cliffside, we cannot attach machinery to our anchors and objectively quantify their strength. In most cases we must trust our ability to assess the probability of failure. On one hand we're talking about a personal judgment rooted in one's level of acceptable risk, and one's ability to accurately assess that risk. If your level of acceptable risk is zero (a ratio never realized in the climbing game), then you'll try and take redundancy, and every aspect of SRENE, further than you need to go, and any anchor short of ten bolts will be a deal breaker. Celebrated American climber Curt Shannon puts it this way: "Boeing 747 aircraft do not have two left wings in spite of the fact that if the single, non-redundant left wing comes off, everyone on board will die. Same thing with the use of a single rope. The point being that it is possible to design an element of a mechanism (such as a wing, or a rope) to a standard of quality where a lack of redundancy is a moot issue."

A succinct assessment, but we'd be traversing off early if we left it at that. The fact is, a climbing rope, a harness, a bar-tacked belay loop, a locking biner and the other nonredundant items we all trust—every one is expertly designed, factory made, subject to rigorous quality control and tested by everyone with a clipboard and too many pens in their vest. These nonredundant items are basically the climbing equivalent of the airplane wing, with a fail probability so small that, as Curt pointed out, their redundancy is a moot point.

Climbing anchors, on the other hand, are routinely fashioned in junk rock by people who little understand the gear or rigging techniques and have no experience in judging critical issues like direction of loading and fall factors. To help compensate for these variables, we foster a mindset and tender a criteria (redundancy) suggesting that you double up whatever you can, whenever you can. Period. We climb on one rope and with one harness; we belay off one tree when the tree is healthy and 10 feet wide; and hating every second of it, we sometimes ARE forced into belaying off one nut. But redundancy is one of our stated goals with all anchors. As one climber put it during an Internet discussion: "The purpose behind redundancy is to save your ass when your assumptions are wrong." Another climber added: "Always keep more than one failure point between you and the reaper. This way you have to screw up twice at the same time to kill yourself." I trust the picture is clear.

That much said, does redundancy only imply that we should double up every nut in the system? Actually it's a little more involved. To understand how anchors actually work, you must learn to consider the anchor beyond it's component parts and appreciate it as a whole, as a mechanical system. In this sense redundancy becomes a much broader concern.

Redundancy asks one basic question: Can any one component of the anchor fail that in turn will cause the whole anchor to fail? Initially most people consider redundancy in terms of primary placements. That is, if there are two or more pieces, then an anchor is redundant, right? Not exactly. SRENE is an evaluation criteria covering the entire anchor system. Two good bolts are redundant, but what if we connect them with one sling? If the sling blows, we're goners. So two bolts connected with one sling is not redundant in terms of the system.

Barring huge trees and colossal blocks, the photos in the next chapter illustrate that all acceptable anchors consist of at least two primary anchors, or two groupings of primary anchors, which could also be called the "legs" of an anchor setup. Redundancy in an anchor normally requires that each of the two primary anchors, or legs, be strong enough to sustain worst-case scenario loading. If one or both of the legs are not strong enough for such loading, then we go after equalization/distribution within a leg, as well as between the legs. By way of overhand knots and clove hitches we sometimes make redundant the arms of the slings clipped to single or multiple primary placements. The photos and commentary demonstrate these points. For now it's instructional to understand what NASA discovered in a study of redundant systems:

A. Assume that one leg of your anchor has a failure potential of one in a thousand.

B. It follows that two equal legs would have a failure rate of one in a million (1,000 x 1,000).

C. Three legs would slightly increase the reliability.

D. Four and up make practically no difference.

The bottom line is clear: Even when the individual components of an anchor have a failure rate of one in a thousand, by simply doubling them up you increase the security by a thousand-fold. This alone is a decisive vote for doubling up and making redundant every component within an anchor matrix.

A last redundancy concern is the maxim that you should never place all of your primary placements in the same feature—be it in one section of crack, behind one flake, etc. For better or worse, this maxim can never be realized across the slab. Many times you have no choice but to arrange an anchor in one crack, especially in granite areas like Yosemite. Nevertheless, for several reasons, the maxim is valid as a basic principle.

In areas of suspect rock, aim to spread the primary placements over a few different features, in case one feature should fail. Know that it's exceptionally rare that a fall will dislodge an entire feature. More commonly, a fall will shear away the rock around where a nut or cam is seated, as opposed to blowing out a section of crack or ripping a whole flake off the wall—though both have happened. Another reason to spread the anchor out is that it is difficult to arrange an acceptably equalized, omnidirectional belay from primary placements arranged solely in a straight up and down crack.

Can you, or must you, achieve redundancy in every situation on the cliffside? No. But as a rule of thumb, redundancy is at the top of the list. Bear this in mind when reviewing the photos, where the theory of redundancy is applied in dozens of ways.

CHAPTER NINE

Belay Anchors

A handful of basic rigging methods cover most anchoring demands, providing you understand a few general principles and learn to improvise on a theme with a variety of instruments (gear). In the past the basic rigging methods included the cordelette, the sliding X and the crafty use of slings and clove hitches. Recent tests, however, have determined that the cordelette is dependable only when the arms of the system are of perfect length. The equalette, a new variation of the cordelette, is showing promise as a viable replacement and has thus far received solid reviews following extensive field testing. No doubt other systems will evolve over time as more climbers try to solve the longstanding problem of achieving redundancy and good equalization with limited extension.

The photos in this chapter show examples of typical anchoring setups. Memorizing the rigging on a given belay anchor doesn't mean you'll be able to (or want to) use the exact same method at a different location. The photos simply allow you to study various setups and develop a working understanding of general principles. When studying the photos, try to quickly recognize what basic technique is used, then consider options and mentally formulate ways you might do things differently.

When building any belay anchor, you'll always face limitations. A leader can take only so much gear on her rack, and it's impossible to predict what gear she will place to protect a given pitch. Whatever gear remains on your rack at the end of the pitch is what you have to efficiently and securely fashion a belay. If you don't thoroughly understand the basic principles, you will struggle to build anchors with limited gear.

BUILDING BELAY ANCHORS—A STEP-BY-STEP PROCESS

Aside from the ability to place sound nuts, cams, etc., adaptability and innovation are keys to rigging stout and convenient setups. Belay anchors can be subjected to

Matt Peer sets out *Across the Universe,* Crawford Notch, New Hampshire.
PHOTO BY STEWART M. GREEN.

high-impact loads, so arranging bombproof belay anchors is absolutely crucial.

Experienced climbers go through a step-by-step process when rigging a belay anchor. First is to determine, so far as you can, the directions of pull that the anchor must resist—for both the climber following the pitch and the leader casting off on the next lead. The directions of pull will influence your rigging choices per building a statically equalized or dynamically equalized anchor system.

After determining the possible directions of pull, locate where you want to belay—what physical location is best for tending the line, what affords the most secure and ergonomic stance, what allows use of the remaining gear on your rack, etc. If adequate primary placements aren't available, consider moving the station higher if possible, or lower if necessary. Often you won't have a choice. There will be only a small shelf or one crack.

Most belay anchors are built around one atomic bombproof nut or SLCD, and that's task number one: setting the strongest, most obvious big nut or camming device you can arrange. If extra stout placements abound, go with the one most handily located, ideally about chest level, where you can remain standing, can hang the rack and can keep an eye on the whole works.

STEP-BY-STEP BELAY ANCHOR

- On popular routes the belay stances/ledges are usually well established (though not always ideal). Belay there.

- Further narrow your belay site down to the most secure, ergonomic and practical position.

- Locate suitable cracks or rock features to fashion a "good enough" belay anchor.

- Set the most bombproof, primary big nut or camming device you can find—preferably a multidirectional placement—and tie yourself off before yelling "off belay."

- Determine the direction(s) of pull for both the climber following the pitch and the leader casting off on the next lead.

- Simply and efficiently shore up the primary placement with secondary anchors.

- Try to set the secondary placements in close, but not cramped, proximity.

- If the rock is less than perfect in quality, spread the anchors out, using several features, to preserve redundancy.

- Using modern rigging techniques, connect the various components of the system together so they function as one unit to safeguard against all possible directions of pull.

- Consider tying into the most bombproof anchor with a clove hitch (to aid adjustability).

- When bringing up a second after leading a pitch, if possible situate your body in line between the anchors and the anticipated direction of pull. Remember ABC: Anchor ➤ Belayer ➤ Climber.

- Also remember KISS: Keep It Simple, Stupid. Avoid overbuilding.

Sometimes you'll have to rig the anchor at your feet, or off to one side, or wherever you can get good placements. Whatever the situation, the priority is to sink that first, bombproof placement. No matter if you're standing on a 10- by 10-foot terrace, clip into this piece before you finish rigging the belay anchor and before you go off belay.

Next, shore up the primary placement with secondary placements, striving to keep the grouping close by, but not so close that they are crowding each other. If the rock quality is less than perfect, spread the anchors out, using several features, to preserve redundancy. Don't put all your eggs in one basket. Try to make the placement closest to you (first to be loaded in event of an upward pull) multidirectional by using an SLCD if possible.

Remember you want an efficient anchor, not simply one that will bear the most impact. The placements should be straightforward to place and remove and should be as centrally located as possible—a nice, tight grouping, as opposed to an entangling web of tackle crisscrossing the station.

Personally, I like to place a minimum of four pieces: three in the downward direction and if the situation requires, one upward placement opposing the primary anchor. Sometimes three are enough, and sometimes that's all you'll get. Anything less is a crapshoot. And accept that sometimes you'll be shooting craps. The rock will not always afford instant and bomber belay anchors. You sometimes have to work at getting anything approaching "good enough."

Once the primary placements are set, you must connect the various components together so they function as one unit. This is often the most critical, and difficult, part of the whole procedure. Several possibilities exist for connecting the

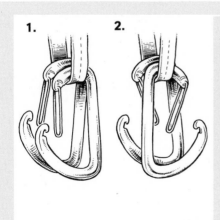

Doubled carabiners should always have the gates opposite and opposed.

1. The wrong way. Even if one of the carabiners is flipped over so the gates are on opposite sides, the gates are still not technically opposed.

2. The right way. Even if one of the biners flipped over and the gates were on the same side, the direction they open would still be in opposition.

anchors, a topic we'll exhaust shortly. For now remember that, if possible, the belayer's body should remain in line between the anchors and the anticipated direction of pull.

Those are the basics. Let's dig into the particulars.

TYING INTO THE BELAY ANCHOR

The standard method of tying into the anchor is via a figure eight on a bight clipped into the *power point* (see upcoming text) with a locking biner, or two biners with the gates opposed. Once a team gets established on a multipitch climb, however, the method of tying in depends on at least two factors: (1) the number of climbers on the team, and (2) whether or not more than one person is doing the leading.

Out in the field you'll see folks tying into the power point with a single clove hitch, two clove hitches, a clove hitch and a figure eight (to multiple power points), a daisy chain, a sling or two or three, an adjustable link of rope and a Ropeman ascender, and countless other methods. Many of these techniques are as sketchy as a felon on bail, none so much as attaching yourself with a daisy chain, which creates a static connection that sacrifices the considerable strength, give and flex offered by tying in with the dynamic climbing rope.

The aim of establishing a protocol on tying in is to facilitate the smooth and secure transition from climbing to belaying to climbing again. If, for instance, a two-person party is swinging leads, the process is fairly straightforward. If you are a three-person party with one person doing the leading, or if the leading and the following is done in no particular order, the belay can quickly become a hateful mess if you don't have a simple and reliable system for tying into the anchor. There are no hard and fast, standardized methods in this work because the configuration of belays is so varied. It will take practice to come up with your own efficient system. There are, however, some basic strategies that work in most instances.

One good strategy is to back up your connection. If you tie into the power point with a clove hitch, tie into another point of the anchor with a figure eight on a bight. The most bomber piece is a good choice for this backup. If you're using a cordelette to connect the anchor pieces, another potential backup point is the "shelf" of the cordelette, which is the point right *above* the power point. This "shelf" also offers an alternative clip-in spot for whoever is leading the next pitch in a group of three or more. The practice results in one less tie-in at the power point, thereby opening it up for others to clip in, and it allows the leader to quickly unclip and take off on the next pitch.

The Enigma of Factor 2 Falls

As we've learned, lab drop tests determined that a factor 2 fall creates the greatest force that can ever be put on a roped safety system. Though we've seen that a real world factor 2 fall generates forces that are less than those registered in the lab drop test, the party line remains the same: If a belay cannot sustain a factor 2 fall, it is not "good enough." And yet the *vast* majority of the most experienced climbers on the planet have little direct experience with a worst-case scenario, factor 2 fall.

American climber and mathematics professor Richard Goldstone puts it this way: "My sense is that circumstances severe enough to result in total anchor failure have happened in the field to no more than a handful of climbers during the nearly forty-nine years I've been climbing." Craig Connally says the same thing another way: "The reason there's so much screwy advice about falls and anchor building is that the roped safety system hardly ever gets stressed to its limits."

If traditional wisdom insists that we build belay anchors to sustain a factor 2 fall, and precious few of our anchors have ever sustained anything close to such loading, on what real world experiences and on what hard information are we basing our recommendations?

While there is a glaring lack of definitive information about real world anchors, this lack is somewhat countered by field testing carried out by millions of climbers annually. Unfortunately for our discussion, but fortunately for climbers, the bulk of this field testing entails fall forces in the factor .3 to .5 range. Better to have a large, controlled database on factor 2 falls that could tell us what techniques worked and what did not so we could base our recommendations on that data. As it stands, we must draw our information from a different, and admittedly, shallower well. That said, we were able to initiate an extensive series of lab tests specifically for this book, and the test results yielded invaluable information about rigging systems. This is only a start, however. Many more tests by many more people are required to wrestle with this very slippery subject.

Spreading the Load

A fall generates forces, and you want the impact of those forces equalized over and absorbed throughout the entire anchor matrix. A wise stockbroker has a broad portfolio. He doesn't toss all his dough into a single fund, no matter how blue the chip. Same thing with belay anchors. We spread the load over several sound primary placements and reduce the possibility that the whole matrix will fail. And that is, and always will be, the primary function of a belay anchor—to hold no matter what.

We've all had pro rip out; some of us have had two points of pro rip out. But it's unlikely you will ever read about a failed anchor that was set in good rock, well-equalized, redundant and fashioned to absorb loading in the direction of the pull. Three or four bomber nuts and SLCDs, judiciously equalized and set in good rock, simply are not going to fail no matter how far a leader might fall on them. Let's make no mistake about it: A leader can generate only so much impact force, and a viable anchor can readily sustain it.

By using oppositional elements in the anchor (if required) and properly equalizing them to the primary, bombproof anchors, the anchor becomes **multidirectional.** You can yank and tug and fall on it from many angles and that baby will still hold. Again, that's the bottom line with a belay anchor—it must hold, no matter what.

While we have stressed the critical importance of getting a secure placement just off the belay—the Jesus Nut—and have clarified that the top placement always sustains the highest loading during a fall, we nevertheless strive to build our anchors to sustain that worst-case scenario fall because if all our pro rips out, we still have a strong and secure anchor to save the day.

But it's a plain fact: No matter how superb the rigging, we almost never attain uniform equalization between primary placements in the anchor matrix. At best we achieve a somewhat even distribution of loading. Knowing that equalization is a relative term does not keep us from striving to build belay anchors with the following features:

- Distributes the load as evenly as possible between the component parts of the anchor system
- Has a minimum of slack between the various tie-in points
- Uses a rigging method and/or multidirectional components capable of self-adjusting, or automatically redistributing the load as the loading direction changes (say, as the belayer shifts position, or the belayed climber pitches off and swings, or if the belayer gets yanked upward)
- Can withstand the greatest load a leader can place upon it

STATIC AND AUTOMATIC EQUALIZATION SYSTEMS

There are two kinds of equalizing systems: static, pseudo-equalizing systems (also called pre-equalized systems) and automatic (dynamic or self-adjusting) systems. The following pages, photos and commentary explore these systems in detail, but to start out, understand these short definitions:

- A **static** equalizing system refers to a grouping of nuts, pitons, bolts, etc., which are tied off together with no slack or adjustability in the system. For example, if we have four nuts in a line and tie them all off with a cordelette, the impact force will, to some degree, get distributed over all four nuts. Realistically, this system provides imperfect equalization, so one of the anchors—the anchor connected to the shortest arm of the rigging system—is inevitably sustaining most of the load.
- An **automatic** equalizing (dynamic/self-adjusting) system employs various sling configurations between the anchors so all pieces share, to greater or lesser degrees, any applied load, even if the loading direction changes. The use of

limiter knots to reduce extension on sliding X configurations creates something of a hybrid anchor between automatic and static equalization, but for the purposes of this book, we will consider those anchors to be part of this category. Sometimes belay anchors feature a combination of automatic and static equalizing constructs. For instance, you might end up with several pairings of nuts equalized with the sliding X, these being lashed together with a cordelette or an equalette to create a complete system.

Modern Rigging Trends

For many years most climbers tied directly into a belay anchor with the lead rope. The rope tie-in was considered the quickest, simplest and least gear-intensive method, and was used ten to one over all other setups. About fifteen years ago the cordelette was invented to spread the load quickly and somewhat evenly between two bomber bolts on sport-climb belay anchors. Over time the cordelette became a popular rigging technique for trad climbing. The notion was to maximize the overall strength of the anchor system, while reducing the belay switch-over time if one climber was leading all of the pitches, or if the party had three or more climbers.

As popular as the cordelette is, recent testing has shown that it does not achieve an acceptable level of equalization when the arms of the system are of unequal lengths. While the cordelette remains a viable rigging system in the equal-arm configuration (connecting two—and only two—placements), the equalette is looking good in both the lab and the field, and it appears to be a logical option when the arms of the rigging system are of unequal length, and even when they are not.

Another rigging method, built on the sliding X, is also a primary rigging strategy. More recently, climbers have started integrating both the cordelette and the sliding X into an anchor matrix. For example, you might equalize several placements with the sliding X, then use the cordelette to statically equalize the power point.

Because the cordelette, sliding X and equalette are primary rigging techniques, it's essential to understand the pros and cons of each. It is here, in this critical discussion, that the SRENE criteria jump to full life, for only when applied can the concepts be made clear. The reason for having started with a discussion of climbing forces (and direction of pull) is to help you make these what-if analyses more concrete. And it's pretty much what-if from here on out.

When to Use What

Trying to establish when to use the equalette, sliding X or cordelette is a slippery business. Recent lab testing has helped establish performance parameters of these

This photo shows decent technique for tying into an anchor the old fashioned way, directly with a rope, which might be necessary if you're short on gear or in some sort of emergency situation. An SLCD and hexentric are tied off tight with clove hitches to a backup SLCD above. The lower SLCD is set as an oppositional piece to hold an upward pull. The belayer is tied into the strand of the rope coming down on the left side of the photo, which will minimize extension if the lowest piece fails. Note that the load strands of the clove hitches are cinched nice and tight, with no strands on the gate of the biner. You might consider belaying the second through a biner connected to one of the upper pieces, especially if you're expecting someone to struggle and hang on the rope.

systems, as opposed to the "traditional wisdom" (oftentimes wrong) that guided our choices in the past. Let's first look at the cordelette, the mother of all rigging methods for more than a decade.

CORDELETTES

Until recent testing showed its shortcomings, a cordelette was generally used to distribute the load between two, three or four (rare) primary placements in a belay anchor. The cordelette minimizes the number of carabiners, slings and quickdraws required to connect the placements in an anchor matrix (unless you just use the rope), thereby justifying its size and weight. A standard cordelette consists of an 18-foot piece of 5.5mm high-tensile cord or 7mm nylon and has been commonly used by guides to create a single point for connecting clients to all the individual anchors of a belay or as a toprope anchor system.

The cordelette is tied into a loop with a triple fisherman's knot (if using high-tensile cord) or a double fisherman's knot (if using nylon cord) and clipped into each of the primary anchors. A loop of the cord is then pulled down between each of the primary pieces. If you have three pieces in your belay anchor, you'll get three loops that must then be pulled tight toward the anticipated loading direction (direction of pull). As a statically equalized system, the cordelette is designed to withstand forces in a specific direction of pull, and that direction must remain constant or the effectiveness of the cordelette is greatly compromised. In short, rigging the cordelette in the direction of anticipated loading is absolutely vital.

Align the fisherman's knot in the cordelette so it is below the highest piece in the matrix, which keeps the bulky fisherman's knot from interfering with the power point knot—a common mistake for beginners. Next, tie an overhand knot, or if you have enough cord, a figure eight knot, near the tie-in point. Clipping a biner in at this point greatly facilitates tying the knot with nice, equal loops. Tie the power point loop about 4 inches in diameter, roughly the same size as the belay loop on your harness. The cordelette has now formed three separate, redundant loops that offer no extension if one of the primary placements fails.

The problem with this configuration is the issue of equalization. Lab tests clearly show that unless the cordelette is configured with perfectly equal-length arms it does not achieve a remotely adequate degree of equalization between the primary placements. Instead the bulk of any loading is absorbed by the shortest arm in the system. Hence the cordelette works best in those situations where it can be configured with equal-length arms and connected to side-by-side placements (such as bolts atop a sport climb), and also where the direction of pull remains a constant—straight up and straight down.

Always connect yourself to the rigging system with a small

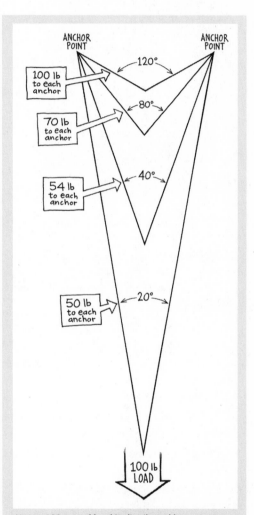

How a 100-pound load is distributed between two anchors rigged at various angles. Whether rigging with a cordelette, equalette or sliding X, the forces on the primary placements increase significantly at greater angles.

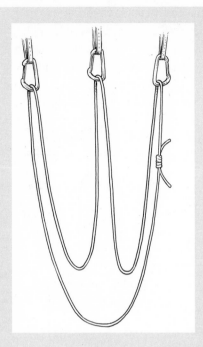

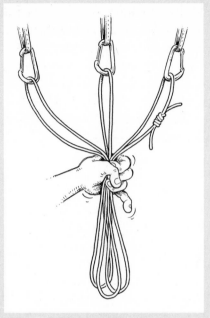

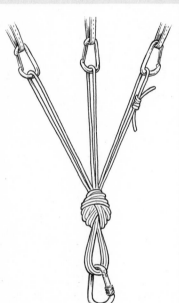

The cordelette attaches multiple anchor points with a single, mostly static tie-in point. Remember to keep the fisherman's knot up out of the way like this. With equal-length arms and a predictable direction of pull (straight up or down), a cordelette like this is a viable anchor choice.

amount of climbing rope. This provides a more dynamic system and allows quick escape if need be. Always make sure the rope remains the primary attachment, owing to it's dynamic (stretch) properties. One disturbing, recent trend (and probably 90 percent of novice trad climbers do this) is to use a daisy chain for your attachment. This static connection—which daisy chain manufacturers warn against—precludes the climbing rope from acting as a shock absorber. In the double fatality on *The Step* at Tahquitz Rock, the belayer was attached to the cordelette with a small length of high-tensile cord, rather than with the main rope. Never do so.

In summary, when the primary placements of the belay anchor are of equal distance from the power point and bomber, and the direction of possible loading (pull) remains constant, a statically equalized setup like the cordelette is a viable choice.

Again, the biggest shortcoming of the cordelette—one that keeps some climbers from using the cordelette at all—is that it loses almost all, if not all, of its equalization properties if the loading direction changes. In short, a cordelette sacrifices equalization properties if it is impacted in a direction for which it is not rigged, and to a lesser degree, in the direction for which it was rigged. On most

A STANDARD CORDELETTE:

- Is a statically equalized system that is most effective when its arms are of equal length.

- Normally consists of an 18-foot piece of 7mm nylon cord (tied into a loop with a double fisherman's knot) or 5.5mm high-tensile cord (connected with a triple fisherman's knot).

TO RIG A CORDELETTE:

- Clip the cordelette into the primary anchors, then pull the loops of cord down between each of the pieces.

- Pull the arms of the cordelette tight toward the anticipated loading direction (direction of pull).

- Align the fisherman's knot so it is below the highest primary placement in the system, free and clear of the power point knot.

- Secure the power point with an overhand knot, or if you have enough cord, a figure eight knot. Tie the power point loop about 4 inches in diameter, roughly the same size as the belay loop on your harness.

- Clip into the power point with a section of the climbing rope, not with a daisy chain or other device made of high-tensile cord.

Belay anchor with three SLCDs tied off with a cordelette. The granite is sound, and all three cams are bomber, well retracted (over 50 percent), with all the cams nicely contacting the walls of the crack. The rope is attached to the power point with two carabiners opposed and reversed (including one locking). Clean, simple and strong. The bottom cam means this anchor could also withstand an upward force.

As our cordelette discussion points out, load equalization over placements set in a vertical crack is much more a concept than a fact. Here the bulk of direct, downward loading will fall on the middle SLCD.

climbs, however, the possible directions of loading are obvious and constant—most often they are pretty much up and down. So to safeguard against a lateral direction of pull when ascending a soaring crack, where lateral forces cannot occur, is to account for theoretical concerns, not real ones.

Limitations? Absolutely. But so long as you understand and work with them, the cordelette works well enough to remain popular. With practice, rigging anchors with cordelettes becomes quick and straightforward.

Cordelettes and Equalization—an Example

Because the cordelette was for many years a favored rigging strategy and because we are now suggesting otherwise in many situations, it is worthwhile to understand the entire picture. You will certainly hear strong recommendations for using the cordelette in all circumstances, especially from those not privy to recent test results and the theoretical discussion that follows.

Professor Richard Goldstone has over the years taken a studied look at some basic assumptions per anchoring mechanics. In the following paraphrased abstract, he presents a theoretical analysis (which testing later confirmed) from which the cordelette may never recover it's reputation for equalization. He wrote:

Imagine three primary placements in a vertical crack connected and "equalized" by a cordelette. In this common setup, providing the three arms of the cordelette are equally tensioned, many climbers assume that any loading is distributed equally between the three placements. However, this assumption is not true in general and may not even be approximately true in simple cases.

Consider the mechanism by which the cordelette transmits forces to the anchor points. When the power point is loaded, the arms of the cordelette stretch a little and the power point lowers relative to the amount of stretch. The tension in each cordelette arm is proportional to the relative stretch of the arms, and the relative stretch of different arms will, in general, be different.

To picture this in

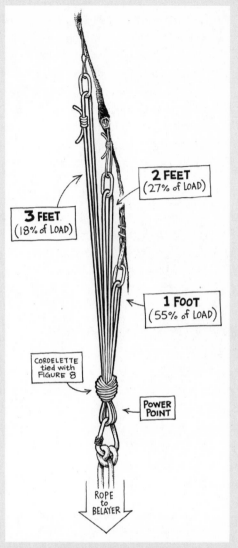

3 FEET
(18% of LOAD)

2 FEET
(27% of LOAD)

1 FOOT
(55% of LOAD)

CORDELETTE
tied with
FIGURE 8

POWER
POINT

ROPE
to
BELAYER

Using a cordelette to connect anchors in a vertical crack results in an anchor that does not come close to truly equalizing the forces.

action, return to our simple and quite prevalent case of three primary placements in a vertical line. Suppose that there is 1 foot from the power point to the lowest anchor, and that each of the two higher anchors is 1 foot above its predecessor. This means that the arms from the power point to the anchors are 1, 2 and 3 feet respectively. When loaded, the power point experiences a downward displacement of e feet (e will typically be a small fraction). The relative displacements are thus e, e/2, and e/3, which means the tension in the 2-foot arm is half the tension in the 1-foot arm, and the tension in the 3-foot arm is one-third the tension in the 1-foot arm. Put another way, the lowest placement takes about 55 percent of the load, the middle placement takes about 27 percent of the load, and the top placement takes about 18 percent of the load. Obviously this contradicts conventional wisdom about so-called anchor equalization, which holds that each anchor takes one-third of the load.

To summarize, Professor Goldstone is pointing out that when the arms of the cordelette are of different length, equalization is compromised by stretch in the arms, with the arm that stretches least in this case bearing better than half (55 percent) of the load. When tested, the cordelette proved to equalize less proficiently than even Professor Goldstone surmised, which is why the cordelette can no longer be recommended for its equalization properties when the arms are of unequal length.

Off-Axis Loading on Cordelettes

So far our examples assume that loading will come from directly below the power point, which gives the cordelette its best chance of equalizing the load evenly between the arms. What happens, then, with load angle changes, when the direction of pull comes from 5 or 10 degrees off the vertical axis? To visualize the vectors involved, consider this paraphrased explanation of Dr. D. F. Merchant, from his excellent cave rescue treatise, *Life on a Line*.

> Whenever you combine two anchors to a single power point (as you do with a cordelette) there will be an angle between them. The smaller this angle, the smaller the load on each anchor when a direct down-load is applied to the power point. If your load pulls outside the angle of your anchors, at least one connection (arm of the cordelette) will be slack, bearing little to no load, with the other connection taut to the load-bearing placement. If your load comes from a fixed direction, minimizing the angle between your anchors is the main aim. If you need a range of motion, then making sure your anchors stay loaded is a compromise against minimizing the angles.

This underscores the fact that with the cordelette, there is only one load angle where force is distributed—in varying percentages—to the anchor pieces. When

Four camming devices in a horizontal crack connected with a cordelette. Note how the fisherman's knot (on the cordelette) is rigged well out of the way. As with all statically equalized anchors, the setup is set for a single direction of pull. Even the slightest oblique angle of pull will load one side of the triangle while the other side will bear little if any load. Stretchy nylon cord is more forgiving in this regard, but off-axis loading will still weight one of the placements over the others. However, because the arms of the cordelette are of equal length here, climbers can expect to achieve some equalization as long as the direction of pull is straight down.

we stray even a few degrees off the loading axis, meaning the direction of pull impacts the cordelette from a different angle than that for which it was rigged, the off-axis loading will tension the left or right arm of the cordelette, which will then bear the brunt, if not all, of the load.

In *The Mountaineering Handbook*, Craig Connally gives a simple numerical example: "Consider a two-placement setup where the legs join at a 30-degree angle. If the load is off the precise balancing direction by 10 degrees, one anchor will take three times the force of the other."

If this off-axis load exceeds the max load of each primary protection point, the pieces will fail in succession—the ghastly cascade failure—as the force shock loads from one arm to the next. If the off-axis loading does not exceed the max strength of the primary protection points, redundancy here applies only as a backup since the load will be held by one piece, not the two or three for which the cordelette was rigged in the first place. (This is not meant to discount the importance of redundancy, which would obviously be critical if the primary load-bearing piece were to fail.)

This brings us back to the matter of stretch in the arms of the cordelette. Specifically, can the stretch of the arms provide some off-axis load sharing? And if

This cordelette has been unknotted and used in the "Web-o-lette" mode. This is a trick adopted by many professional guides to add greater utility to their cordelette. When untied, the cord works well for connecting three points when a standard cordelette, describing a single loop, would be too short. Simply tie the ends with figure eights, clip into the two outside anchor points in a V configuration, take the middle bight and clip it into a third point. Then gather the two bights together and tie a two-loop power point with a figure eight.

In this particular setup, all three camming devices are bomber, and the granite sound. Notice the upper left camming device has a sling looped through in the "basket" mode, to prevent the carabiner from grinding on the edge of the crack. The lower left cam-ming device has a locking carabiner to prevent the gate opening on the crack edge, and a slight improvement here would be to do the same at the upper right cam. While there is some loss of strength in those arms of the cordelette with a single strand, this rig—based on bomber primary placements—is a trade off most climbers can live with.

As is always the case with such setups, this is rigged for a downward pull, and any oblique loading will put the load on one of the other three primary placements. Also, because the arms of the cordelette are of unequal length, true equalization is not achieved.

so, to what extent would the stretch increase the ability of the cordelette to more evenly distribute the load over three pieces placed in a vertical axis as well as increase the loading axis when the primary placements are on a horizontal or slanting axis?

So far we've see that the random changes in the cordelette's arm length may well result in limited initial loading on at least one primary placement as the anchor matrix is loaded and the stretching process begins. If high-tensile cord (an almost static material) is used, then it is possible that at least one anchor will never be loaded unless there is a failure in the others.

This means that Professor Goldstone's example (three placements in a vertical crack), where the long arm of a cordelette absorbs 18 percent of the load, could be a high estimate. "In fact," writes Goldstone, "my suspicion is that for many anchors with three or more pieces in any configuration, it is quite possible that nearly all the load will be imparted to a single anchor, even if the load comes from the expected direction."

The fact is that any static equalization setup is more realistically an example of redundancy than an example of equalization. We should always keep that in mind when we're building an anchor with a cordelette. Other valuable feedback comes from Jim Ewing, the quality control manager for Sterling Ropes, who noted during testing that low-stretch high-tensile cord always weighted one leg first, which failed, then the next leg, which failed, then finally the last leg, which failed.

Bottom line:

1. A no-extension anchor (including the cordelette) is a distributed anchor, not an equalized one, and it is possible that at least one of the anchor pieces will experience little or no load (unless others fail).

2. The ability to distribute forces to all anchors is increased by the use of stretchier material, a strong endorsement for using a 7mm nylon (nylon) for any rigging system.

Point 2 is commonly trotted out by those recommending the cordelette for all anchoring setups. They claim that cord stretch provides off-axis load sharing, and it might somewhat, but the question becomes this: What available material provides the ratio of stretch best suited to promote load sharing on a shock-loaded cordelette? An answer comes again from Jim Ewing at Sterling Ropes, who tested two cordelette setups (hand tied), one with high-tensile cord, the other with low-tech nylon (nylon). In these tests the nylon always won. The stretchy nylon not only won, it provided a much more dynamic system, something mostly lost on a cordelette rigged with comparatively static high-tensile cord.

HIGH-TENSILE CORD VS. NYLON

For those interested in the actual figures of the Sterling tests, the high-tensile cord failed at 5,000+ pounds, with nylon holding strong to roughly 7,000 pounds, even though it's rated to only 2,500 pounds. Note that the 7,000-pound mark was attained because loops of nylon have a doubling effect in their capacity (a looped leg of 2,500-pound test fails close to 5,000 pounds, while a looped leg of high-tensile cord still fails at 5,000 pounds, not 10,000 as you would expect). In the widely reviewed Moyer study (see below), the high-tensile cord in both the weak and strong arm failed at just over 4,000 pounds.

This article is definitely worth reviewing:

2000 International Technical Rescue Symposium: "Comparative Strength of High-Strength Cord" by Tom Moyer, Paul Tusting and Chris Harmston

(Chris Harmston was quality assurance manager at Black Diamond)

www.xmission.com/~tmoyer/testing

THE SLIDING X

With the advent of the sliding X (aka crossed sling, magic X), the concept of dynamic equalization was born. To most every trad climber's relief, the sliding X apparently resolved two long-standing concerns: (1) how to achieve maximum equalization between two primary pieces of protection, and (2) how to safeguard against changes in the direction of loading. Functionally effective within a wide axis, the sliding X can be loaded from various directions, and the "X" will dynamically shift to help distribute the force between two pieces.

Rigging the Sliding X

The sliding X is simple to construct, but a proper twist in the sliding X sling is essential. When you bungle twisting the X into the sling, the sliding X is totally useless if one placement fails. To confirm proper rigging after connecting the sliding X to the placements, simply clip a biner into the X, weight the placements and slide the biner back and forth along the sling to ensure fluid and stately functioning.

The sliding X provides true automatic equalization; the drawback is that it can allow extension in the system if the slings are long and one of the anchors fails. To minimize the potential extension in longer slings, tie an overhand "limiter" knot in the long leg of the sling, just above the tie-in point. (Keep in mind that this limiter knot, while it reduces the possibility for extension, also by its very nature limits the equalization properties of the sliding X.) Make sure the angle between the two legs of the sling is not too large. If the angle is larger than about 45 degrees, use a longer sling to decrease the angle and avoid load multiplication. An angle of about 25 degrees, as shown in the sliding X drawing, works well.

While it's an ingenious, simple and effective rigging method, the main concern is that the sliding X violates the No Extension criteria of SRENE. Put simply, the sliding X is used to connect two primary placements. If one of the two primary anchors should blow when loaded, the force would "extend" or drop onto the remaining placement equidistant to the slack in the sling. The concern is that the force dumping onto the second piece might possibly produce cascade zippering of the remaining pieces of the anchor. The possibility of this has always remained a black mark against the sliding X, but Craig Connally (along with recent testing) largely disproved the prevailing paranoia about the minimal extension (with the limiter knots) possibilities with the sliding X.

Basically Connally explains that true shock loading cannot occur. Mirroring recent testing done by Duane Raleigh at *Rock & Ice* magazine, he provides the example of a climber who clips to an anchor with a Spectra daisy chain, climbs a few feet past the anchor, then falls. The Spectra daisy means there's no energy-

The sliding X equalizes an anchor dynamically when the load changes directions.

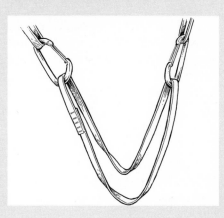

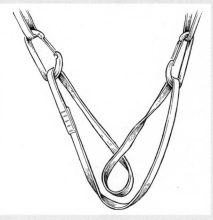

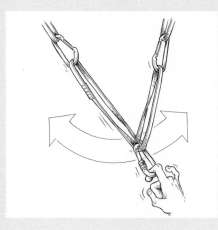

absorbing rope in the system, Connally says, "and forces rise incalculably high. In real-life situations where this has happened, hardware has broken and climbers have fallen to their deaths." That's true shock loading. But in the case of moderate extension found in the failed arm of a sliding X anchor, the aforementioned shock loading does not occur if there's dynamic rope in the system. An example would be to picture a climber hanging on 10 feet of rope. A placement blows and drops him a foot. Disaster? Unlikely, since that amounts to a fall factor 0.1, which is less than the average of around 0.3 for most climbing falls. Granted, you avoid building anchors that could result in really long extension, but there's little cause to fear ordinary setups.

SLIDING X BASICS:

- The sliding X is an automatic equalizing system.
- It is normally rigged on standard length and/or double-length sewn slings.
- A proper twist in the sliding X sling is essential to prevent failure of the complete system if one piece pulls. Always double-check to be sure that this twist is in place.
- After connecting the sliding X to the placements, clip a biner into the X, weight the placements and slide the biner back and forth along the sling to ensure fluid functioning.
- To minimize potential extension in longer equalizing slings, tie an overhand limiter knot in the long leg of the sling, just above the tie-in point.
- To avoid load multiplication, keep the angle between the two legs around 25 degrees (or less). If the angle is larger than about 45 degrees, use a longer sling to decrease the angle.

Sliding X: Normal Usage

Let's look closely at how the sliding X is normally engaged and draw some rules of thumb for general usage.

With solid, two-bolt anchors on multipitch sport climbs (where the issue of extension is diminished and the scale tips toward equalization or redundancy), setup is quick and easy. Plus, the sliding X saves having to leave two draws at the anchor. And for anchors placed in non-horizontal orientations—say, two cams in a slanting crack—the sliding X can connect the pair so they are largely equalized while providing vastly more multidirectional capacities than if you were to tie the same two pieces together with either a cordelette or with knots tensioned in a sling. In fact, whenever you wish to dynamically distribute the load between two pieces, the sliding X is both effective and the best-known method.

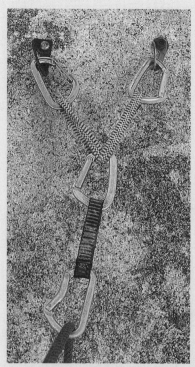

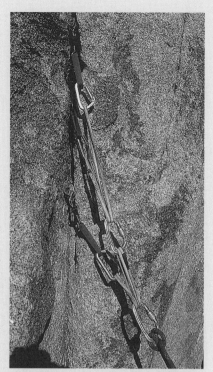

A sliding X connecting two bolts. This self-equalizing technique can be used when leading if the need arises to spread potential loading over two sketchy bolts placed close together, or two marginal pieces of gear.

A three-piece anchor equalized with sliding X's. The lower sling has been doubled to adjust the location of the power point.

The sliding X is also effective for equalizing pieces on lead, especially when doubling up small or sketchy nuts, when it is desirable to get load distribution over both pieces. Likewise when arranging protection before a traverse, or after a traverse, when the route goes abruptly up, the sliding X is a blessing, equalizing marginal pieces so they reinforce each other across a multidirectional range. The possibility of extension (small with limiter knots) here is eclipsed for ease of setup when out on the sharp end.

A leader will also find the sliding X useful as a power point on multipitch routes. For instance, at the end of a lead, if you gain a ledge and need to move around, the sliding X will always keep tension on the anchor and retain equalization.

Occasionally the "X" in the configuration can bind on itself (the so-called "clutch effect"). A simple and test-proven solution is to rig the power point with one or two

Here we have a pre-equalized anchor, meaning no self-equalizing sliding X is used. The primary placements are tied with Dyneema slings, shortened and pre-equalized by tying limiter knots. This anchor is rigged for a downward pull only. The equalization looks tight, and even though it's impossible to achieve the best equalization with such a static system, this anchor could easily hold two tons. Once loaded, however, even under body weight, those thin slings will be *very* difficult to unknot, particularly at the overhand knots.

pear-shaped anodized biners. This eliminates the clutch effect and allows the X to slide freely on the sling, enhancing equalization.

Good, Bad and Both

What pairs of placements are best exploited by the sliding X, and which placements, if any, call for a different rigging strategy? Placement quality spans a wide spectrum, but there are three basic pairings: (1) two good primary placements,

Here we have the same anchor as shown on the previous page, except now the three pieces are self-equalized with two sliding X knots. Unlike the previous anchor, if the load angle changes on this set up, the anchor will remain equalized. The limiter knot tied into the right-hand sling just above the power point will limit extension if the right piece should fail. However, the knot also serves to limit the equalization potential of this anchor—as with every set up, compromises are part of the deal.

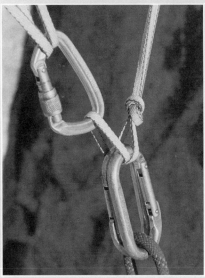

Close-up of previous photo. An overhand limiter knot is tied on the right side of the sliding knot to check extension if the piece should fail.

Three camming devices equalized with a sliding X and clove hitches. This is a good belay anchor rig for a multipitch climb, providing the two climbers are swinging leads. Since there is no power point, climbers swapping leads at this belay stance will require the arriving climber to also rig his rope in this fashion. No big deal, but a bit more time consuming, and a real cluster if there were a third climber at this stance. If one of the two CDs on top were to blow out, there would be sudden loading on the remaining anchor; but judging by the placements (A-1), this would be nearly impossible, even in a factor 2 fall situation, as the downward force would be shared by the two cams, and the force required to break the sling would be astronomical.

(2) two bad placements, and (3) one good and one bad placement.

With poor (i.e., weak) placements, the concern is that a fall could blow out the anchor point, so equalization becomes a priority. The aim is to reduce the initial loading on the stacked (doubled up), weak placements by distributing the load as equally as possible over both pieces. Here, extension is of less concern than maximizing the potential holding strength of the anchor point to the extent that it will actually hold. Clearly two sketchy placements are better than one. And since the sliding X is the best thing going for equalizing two placements—especially with the use of limiter knots—it remains for many the strategy of choice when rigging together stacked, sketchy placements.

Most climbers in the no-extension camp avoid the sliding X unless the primary placements are bomber. When the placements are mediocre to poor, many will statically equalize using overhand knots on a sling, a method that testing has shown to yield little—if any—equalization between pieces. It should be noted that the general anchor preference for those in the no-extension camp is Redundancy

Same anchor as previous page, now rigged to be entirely self-equalizing. An overhand limiter knot tied on the left side of the upper sling (configured in a sliding X) would limit extension if the top cam failed. This rig, in turn, is equalized with two slings paired up and attached (via a sliding X) to the lower piece, to safeguard against an upward/outward pull on the anchor.

Deceptively clean, simple and effective, it normally takes a leader some time to A) survey a given belay and quickly decide upon such a system, and B) quickly and efficiently rig same. While its utility has been proven over several decades, initial work with the sliding X is sometimes confusing. Ultimately there are but a few tricks to using the sliding X, including the limiter knots to reduce extension. Much of the process is simplified once you can quickly determine what sized slings are needed for a given setup, as well as your ability to shorten the slings as needed. Using, or trying to use, oversize slings—which adds needless slack in the system—is a common error when first employing the sliding X. As with all anchor building, confidence and efficiency comes with practice.

and Approximate Equalization with No Extension. For those less concerned about extension, it's better to dynamically equalize the load on the gear (using the sliding X) in an effort to prevent failure than to anticipate failure and mitigate the consequence of extension. Using limiter knots to minimize extension in a sliding X is a solution that could possibly appease both camps, but as yet, it has not.

Changes in the Direction of Pull

Although this was covered in earlier chapters, it's worth repeating: Every climber having to hand build a belay anchor on a route that traverses left or right directly off the belay faces a particularly challenging situation. Pitons, fixed pins and (to a lesser degree) SLCDs are all multidirectional, but everything else is unidirectional, so any multidirectional capacities must be provided by the rigging.

Consider, for example, a belay anchor where the leader traverses 10 feet right, places a nut and falls. Providing the protection holds, the direction of pull will come directly from the right. If the protection fails, or if the leader falls before placing the initial pro, the direction of pull will describe an arc. Much of the load comes when the leader's straight-down fall begins to be pulled into the arc, and it continues until he is in the fall line.

Here the challenge is to build an anchor that will safeguard dead lateral pull, the arc of the swing and the straight down loading once the leader's full weight slams onto the end of the rope. A statically equalized anchor can only cover this 90-degree arc at various points. At best the load will fall variously onto individual placements as the climber swings through the arc. A dynamically equalized anchor like the sliding X—alone, or as a component within a larger anchor matrix—can cover the entire arc insofar as the X slides as the vectors change.

THE EQUALETTE

The equalette was born out of lab tests conducted by Jim Ewing at Sterling Ropes. The system was rigorously field tested by professional guides Bob Gaines, Tom Cecil and others, who reported very favorable results. While only time can render the verdict on a rigging system, the equalette and quad (explained shortly) performed well in both the lab tests and in the field, and they are worth consideration as primary rigging tools.

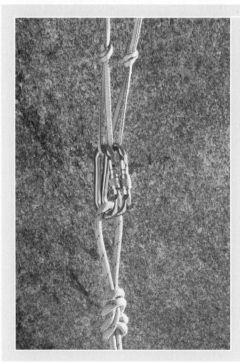

This close up of an equalette power point (tied using slings rather than cord) clearly shows how to rig two locking biners through the strands between the limiter knots. The belayer is tied into the power point with a figure eight knot. This set up will remain equalized if the load swings right or left, but if one anchor should fail, the limiter knots will minimize extension in the system.

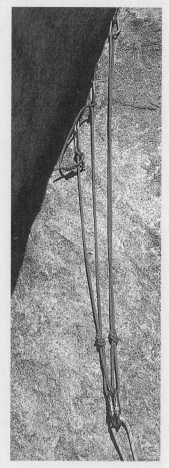

Three-piece anchor rigged with an equalette. Not only solidly equalized but able to adjust to changes in loading direction.

Three-piece anchor rigged with an equalette.

Basically an equalette is built on a cordelette, and field testing has suggested a 20-foot piece of 7mm nylon cord works well in situations ranging from multipitch ice climbs to trad multipitch setups to short sport routes. After the cord is connected with a double fisherman's knot, the loop is then formed into a U shape. At the bottom of the U, two limiter knots are tied approximately 10 inches apart, with the fisherman's knot situated just above one of the limiter knots. This keeps the fisherman's knot clear of the two-strand arms of the equalette that are used to tie off primary placements. For speed and efficiency the limiter knots are best left tied into the sling between usage.

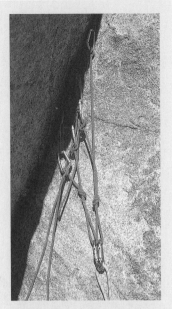

A four-piece equalette rig. Four placements in a vertical crack usually result in a complicated and messy rigging system. Here everything is simple and clean, with good equalization between the two arms and some load sharing between the strands of each arm. While it is unrealistic to think any rigging system can equally load four placements, this equalette comes as close as you will likely get when using a single sling to connect four placements.

Four-piece equalette rig. Very simple and very stout.

Between the two limiter knots are two strands; the power point is rigged by clipping two locking biners into the individual strands—one locker for each strand (see photos).

The equalette can be used to connect two, three or four primary placements and is especially effective in rigging vertically oriented placements, as found in a vertical crack. When rigging, keep the power point centered at the bottom by clipping the lowest placement first then working up the placements from there.

To start, hold the right-hand limiter knot 2 to 6 inches below your lowest piece. (When rigged, an equalette will always feature a right- and left-side orientation). Imagine you are starting by tying into the "right side" of the anchor. After clipping

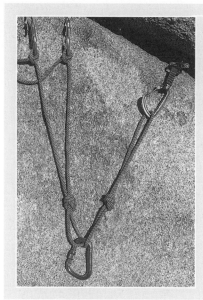

Three-piece anchor connected with an equalette. This system is clean, simple and well equalized. When only using one locking biner at the power point, clip it through one strand, then twist the other strand 180 degrees and clip into it. The technique is the same as clipping into a sling to form a Sliding X.

into the piece or set of pieces on the right, hold the left-side limiter knot even with the first knot, and clip into the piece or pieces on the left. Adjust the strands so your knots end up evenly tensioned (clove hitches are very helpful there, if not required).

For a two-placement setup, connect each arm of the equalette to the placements via the loops in the cord, clove hitches or overhand knots on a bight. For three placements, one arm will accommodate two placements (usually with clove hitches tied into individual strands of the arms), and the other arm will connect to one placement (via the loop in the cord, a clove hitch or overhand on a bight). For connecting four placements, each strand (four total) of the two arms will connect the placements via the loop in the cord, clove hitches. Be sure the load-bearing strands align with the spine of the biner.

The equalette can also be rigged using a double-length sling, though you'll find the 7mm cordelette easier and more versatile to work with, especially when tying clove hitches. Plus you have the added benefit of the stretch in the nylon cord to reduce peak loading on the anchor system.

Tests show that the equalette allows nearly perfect equalization between the two arms, and it allows a ratio of equalization between both strands on each arm. While it is impossible (in a practical sense) to achieve perfect equalization between all four placements, the equalette achieves a degree of equalization—along with solid redundancy and very inconsequential extension—to a higher degree than any system tested.

Because the power point biners can slip side to side on the strands between the limiter knots, the system, when weighted, will dynamically equalize to accommodate a limited degree of off-axis loading. In those rare cases where horizontal forces can impact the belay, oppositional anchors are needed.

As with any new rigging system, it takes a few times working through a variety of anchors before you can rig the equalette quickly and efficiently. The hardest part of the system is getting used to feathering the knots to achieve equal tension in the arms and/or strands. But this is mastered quickly, making the equalette as fast to rig as the cordelette. And because you don't use as many knots with the equalette, breaking down the system is much faster than breaking down a cordelette.

Advantages of the Equalette

- It provides vastly superior equalization over the cordelette.

- If you pull considerably off-axis on an equalette, two arms remain equalized. With the cordelette, any off-axis loading results in only one strand or arm being loaded.

- It has increased versatility. Given the same length of cord (20 feet), an equalette

---

TYING THE EQUALETTE:

Use 20 feet of 7mm nylon cord tied into a loop with a double fisherman's knot, or 5mm high-tensile cord tied with a triple fisherman's knot.

Form a U shape and grab the cordelette at the bottom of the U.

Position the fisherman's knot about 18 inches above the bottom of the U.

Tie an overhand knot on each side of your palm where you have grabbed the cord, about 10 inches apart.

USING THE EQUALETTE:

At the power point, always use two locking biners, with one locker connected into each separate strand of the power point (between the limiter knots). If you are forced to use one biner, clip one strand, twist the other 180 degrees, then clip the other strand to maintain redundancy. This is the same technique used to clip into a sliding X.

Before using the equalette, make sure you have mastered the clove hitch.

On multipitch climbs (with a two-climber team) where the first climber to the stance is going to lead the next pitch, each climber can clip into the power point with his own two locking biners. If the second climber to the stance is going to lead the next pitch, he can clip a locking biner directly into the two-locking-biner power point (biner to biner). This greatly facilitates secure and speedy turnover at the belay.

allows you to clip off four primary placements, whereas with the cordelette you can usually only clip off three.

- It is fast and easy to rig—and faster to break down—than a cordelette.
- The dual power point facilitates a fast and easy clip-in, even when weighted, resulting in smoother belay transitions.
- Clove hitches are faster and easier to untie than the overhand and figure eights used in other rigging systems
- By leaving the limiter knots fixed in the sling, you gain all the function without the tedious and time-consuming repetition of tying multiple overhand knots at each belay.

Limitations of the Equalette

No rigging method is without its limitations, and one size, or one system, does not fit all circumstances. Initial experiences suggest that the equalette is quite versatile and user friendly, but several things should be kept in mind. While the two arms of the equalette achieve a remarkable degree of equalization, the equalization between the individual strands is less than the almost perfect equalization between the arms when the system is rigged to three or four placements. Also, too many clove hitches tied into small-diameter cord can twist the rope, so consider using a combination of knots when rigging three or more placements.

The Quad

The quad is simply a doubled equalette, resulting in a four-strand "super sling" that has proved peerless for use when belaying and/or toproping from two horizontally oriented (side-by-side) bolts. The quad is a specialty item that has limited practical use, but for those who toprope or belay off bolts, having a quad pre-rigged on a sling means you have a virtually indestructible, ready-made rigging system that almost perfectly equalizes two placements and is rigged as quickly as you can clip off four biners.

The quad is best rigged with 5.5mm high-tensile cord (for durability and compactness). First, form a loop by connecting a 20-foot piece of high-tensile cord with a triple fisherman's knot. Double that loop and form the doubled loop into a U. Tie permanent limiter knots, roughly 10 inches apart, in the bottom of the U (giving you four strands of cord between the two overhand limiter knots). Clip off the doubled ends of each arm to each bolt respectively, and arrange the power point via two lockers clipped into two or three strands between the limiter knots.

The quad is mega-strong and durable, and it provides great equalization, accommodates some off-axis loading and is almost instantaneous to rig. For connecting two side-by-side bolts, the quad is hard to beat.

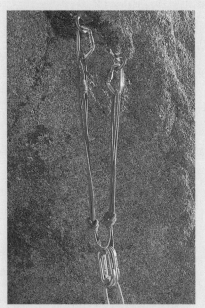

Two-bolt "quad" rig for toprope setup. Lab testing suggests that for two horizontally oriented anchor points (as shown here), the quad setup is basically indestructible. Field testing suggests that for those who frequently belay from, or toprope off, two horizontally oriented bolts (as found on top of countless sport and toprope climbs), a quad rig is your best friend. Simply keep it rigged (with the limiter knots tied) on a piece of 7mm nylon, like this, or 5mm high-strength cord, and break it out for use in these situations. Brute strength and fantastic equalization are achieved just as quickly as you can clip off the bolts and the power point.

Quad rig close-up. At 5,000-pound test for each strand, clipping just two strands at the power point gives you twice the strength ever needed. Clip three and have a submarine anchor.

COMPOSITE ANCHORS: CORDELETTE, SLIDING X AND EQUALETTE

Before the Sterling Ropes tests (described later in this chapter), which redefined our use of the traditional cordelette rigging system, many climbers believed that the sliding X was best considered as a component and that the cordelette was the Whole Ball Game. In any event, because it is fast and requires nothing beyond a sling, the sliding X is the most efficient and flexible method of combining two primary placements to a cordelette, or better yet, an equalette.

In the traversing scenario mentioned earlier, a cordelette or knotted slings would be oriented for a vertical/downward pull. As has been shown, horizontal loading would variously fall on single placements, introducing greater loading/cascade failure potential. In the past it was here that we might have combined a sliding X with a cordelette so that if the leader fell from above the belay with no gear in, the whole anchor was equalized for a downward pull, but if the leader fell on the traverse, the two pieces connected by the sliding X would share the load. Now it seems that we have even more options, including an equalette, or an equalette combined with a sliding X, the latter configuration shorn up with one or more oppositionals set for upward forces, thus forming a super multidirectional anchor. Whatever system or combination you choose, safeguarding the full range of the arc is the goal.

Multi-pitch anchor with cordelette and sliding X combo. While this setup—and ones like it—have been a mainstay for many years, incorporating new techniques such as the equalette will allow climbers to achieve even greater equalization.

Another common composite-anchor situation occurs when a cordelette or equalette isn't long enough to equalize three pieces and remain pointed in the anticipated direction of pull. To fix this, simply equalize two of the pieces with a sliding X, then rig this with the cordelette or equalette to the third piece. In this situation it makes sense to use an equalette in place of a cordelette to achieve superior equalization.

WHAT'S BEST FOR BEGINNERS?

What, by and large, is the most appropriate system for beginners? Every instructor knows that beginners are sure to place sketchy gear (primary placements) and misjudge the direction of pull. For this reason we suggest a self-equalizing system that will adapt to changes in load direction and that will exploit the collective strength of less than textbook placements.

SRENE Anchors

- Solid
- Redundant
- Equalized
- No Extension

Guide Tom Cecil says, "It is more protective to teach self-equalization to beginners. Using self-equalization as a strategy is like using training wheels on a bike. They allow the beginner to lean in any direction and still be held. Over time they learn to anticipate these forces."

Bob Gaines, co-author and owner of Vertical Adventures guide service, sees it this way: "The key in teaching novices is to stress the absolute importance of avoiding factor 2 fall situations. They must be taught to recognize the forces and place pro (the Jesus Nut) soon and often above a belay. This helps ensure that the peak forces that novices encounter will occur at the highest piece of pro, not at the anchor. In most situations, when belayers are catching a leader fall, it is a good thing if the force generated by the falling leader is great enough to pull the belayer slightly upward, as the counterweight effect greatly reduces the force on the piece the leader has fallen on. *Therefore, the best belay strategy is to be anchored against the upward pull with a bit of slack in the system, which provides some counterbalance shock-absorbing, but not so much so that the belayer is pummeled into the wall or extruded through the Jesus Nut.*

"As far as toprope setups go, the direction of pull is basically straight down—easy to judge even by the novice. The biggest and most common mistake I see with novice riggers (aside from poor primary placements) is usually major extension potential and lack of redundancy."

UPWARD OPPOSITIONAL ANCHORS

As shown in various photos, for an anchor to sustain upward loading, we often place a nut or cam set for an upward pull, below and in opposition to the other primary placements in the anchor matrix. While upward forces at a belay are generally small compared to downward forces, I've repeatedly seen this opera play out in the gym: A belayer is grossly outweighed by some lug climbing on a toprope. From neglect or sloth the svelte belayer has foregone a ground anchor. Jumbo pitches off and the belayer is directly wrenched 5 to 20 feet into the air. I've witnessed belayers hoisted all the way to the top anchor, 30 feet up. Jumbo, who is now on the ground, acts as a counterweight/anchor, and the belayer returns to the deck by rappelling down the rope via their belay device, through which the rope runs.

This scenario is particular to the gym, where the routes are vertical to overhanging and the toprope usually runs over a chubby pipe on the top of the route. On a cliff the rope runs through carabiners, at radically tighter angles that won't allow such a meteoric hoist as found in the gym fiasco. Nevertheless, this extravagant hoisting of the belayer often took place during drop tests conducted by the Sierra Club and other outfits during the 1960s and early 1970s.

In the Sierra Club version, one end of some goldline rope was attached to a bucket of concrete weighing roughly 120 pounds. The rope ran up an overhanging wall to an anchor on top—or was connected to a cross-beam in a gymnasium, as the case may have been—then back down to a belayer on the ground. By means of another line, the bucket was heaved 10 to 20 feet into the air—according to the sadistic leanings of the instructor—then cut loose, leaving the belayer to arrest the 10- to 20-foot "fall" via a hip belay. More than one corn-fed male was launched as if shot from a catapult, and it was even money that a wispy female could get extruded halfway through the anchor biner. Such was the examination to become a certified rock climber in years past.

The tubby/svelte toprope hoist job and the antique drop test are goofball examples but nonetheless demonstrate the power of upward forces, and the need to safeguard against them if and when they are significant factors. The question is: What are the circumstances in which upward forces are great enough to warrant oppositional placements in the belay anchor? Let's place ourselves back on the rock and see what questions arise.

Consider a leader climbing above a hanging belay. If she falls off and is arrested by the Jesus Nut, for instance, or pro she has placed higher, the belayer will be pulled upward, or directly toward the first piece of protection off the belay—which is generally upward since most climbs go up. But what is the actual power of this upward force on a belayer? Most of us have held leader falls that have jerked us skyward hard and fast, but even on steep sport routes, if the belayer and the leader weigh roughly the same, when have you ever seen a belayer, following a leader fall, left in midair, stretched taut against an anchor straining against the upward force?

UPWARD FORCE OPPOSITIONALS ARE REQUIRED:

- When a belayer is significantly lighter than the active climber
- Whenever belaying below an overhang and the initial protection off the belay anchor (the Jesus Nut) is directly above or even behind (such as with a roof crack) the anchor
- Where the rock is steep or overhanging and the forces generated by a leader fall can create significant (say, more than 18 inches) "lift" of the belayer

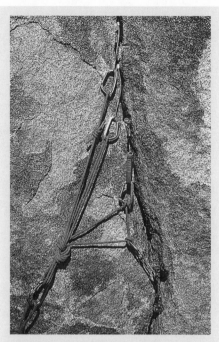

This rig shows a cordelette used to equalize the load on two tapers with another SLCD placed to provide opposition. A belayer tied tight to these anchors isn't going to be lifted any more than 18 inches—enough to provide some "give" in the system, but not enough to be dangerous.

Consequently, in real world climbing, nuts placed in opposition to safeguard against upward forces are never expected to sustain the same loading as those placed for downward forces. In fact one of the ongoing debates in the climbing community is whether or not upward-oppositional placements are necessary at all. Some people favor forgoing upward force oppositionals because they think oppositionals waste time, energy and gear while "needlessly" complicating the system.

Proponents of oppositional anchors raise the possibility of the anchor being uprooted when the belayer is dragged upward in the course of holding a fall. For this to ever happen, the belay anchor would have to be set in vertical cracks and consist of nuts and, less likely, cams—pro that might conceivably be plucked clean if the belayer were yanked a sufficient distance above the anchor. I've never read of an instance where a belayer actually got dragged above the anchor and where the primary placements in the belay anchor itself were plucked from the crack like cloves from a holiday ham.

We know that during a leader fall (held by pro above the belay), slight lift of the belayer's body and flex and give in the system act as peak force reducers, absorbing much of the fall's kinetic energy before the anchor is ever loaded. If nothing else, rope slip/stretch will likely preclude a meteoric hoist, even when little rope is out.

But that's with a belayer who weighs roughly the same as the leader. Get a leader who weighs twice as much as the belayer, and the lift factor becomes significant no matter the angle. Here the peak force reduction enjoyed by the body of a large climber is null and void. And so is the main argument against setting nuts for an upward pull: No matter the fall scenario, the belayer is not likely to be lifted far enough to threaten the anchor. My counter to this claim is that I (210 pounds) once fell at Tahquitz and pulled belayer Lynn Hill (105 pounds) 10 feet into the air.

When Oppositionals Are Required

While there are instances—primarily on low-angled climbs—that climbers can argue against setting nuts to safeguard against upward pull, there are other instances where upward oppositionals are compulsory. These include A) steep hanging belays built from hand-placed gear, B) whenever you are belaying below an overhang and the initial protection off the belay anchor (Jesus Nut) is directly above or even behind (such as with a roof crack) the anchor, and C) when a belayer is significantly lighter than the active climber. All three of these examples are where the rock is near, at or past vertical, where a falling climber will basically be airborne and where forces generated by a leader fall are great enough to start replicating the mega-hoist seen in our first two examples—the toprope scenario in the gym and in the Sierra Club drop test.

Bottom line: Some little "lift" at the belay is usually a good thing, acting as a counterweight and load limiter to the forces generated by a leader falling above. But whenever the potential of that lift exceeds a foot or so (the A, B and C in our examples above), oppositional placements should always be incorporated into the belay anchor.

BELAY POSITIONS

No matter what system you use to connect your primary placements to a power point, the techniques used to arrange various types of belays (direct, semi-direct and re-directed) remain much the same. Although a cordelette is used in these examples, it just as easily could be another type of system or a combination of systems.

Here the belay device is clipped into the belay loop on the climber's harness—an **indirect belay**. Providing the belayer has a solid stance to brace against downward loading, the indirect belay is the technique of choice if the anchor is less than superb. In holding a fall, the belayer bears the brunt of the fall force, which can be uncomfortable and awkward when the falling climber hangs on the rope for a long period of time.

Though this setup is adequate for the low-angled slab it is servicing, if the terrain below was vertical (meaning higher loading), the belayer's backside might get dragged down to a position directly below the anchor. Remember that when the system is loaded, gravity pulls every object on the rope into the fall line, into a position directly below the anchor. Here we have a classic trade-off: In terms of managing forces, the best position for the belayer is directly below the anchor, where downward loading can only pull him straight down. But here the best body position is slightly to the left of the anchor—meaning his arse and brisket will have to bear the bulk of the loading. If the loading becomes greater than what he can maintain (very unlikely on this slab toprope setup), downward loading will pull him down and across to where he is directly beneath the anchor.

Though not always possible, the ideal is: With any indirect belay, the belayer should try to get into a position directly beneath the belay anchor to avoid getting dragged there by downward loading. Remember ABC positioning for bringing up the second: Anchor ──➤ Belayer ──➤ Climber.

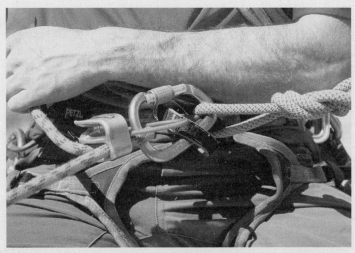

Here the belay device is clipped into both the harness's belay loop *and* the loop in the figure eight tie-in knot. If the climber falls, most of his weight goes onto the anchor, *not* on the belayer—providing that the belayer is situated directly beneath the anchor. To the extent that the belayer is to one side or the other of the anchor is the extent that his body, not the anchor, will bear the load.

This shows how a **re-directed belay** is set up. Always remember that a re-direct basically doubles the loading on the anchor—no problem with premium anchors (like bolts on a sport climb), but with sketchy anchors, a re-directed belay is a little dicey.

This effectively illustrates a clean and simple rigging of a **direct belay.** Whenever the primary placements in the anchor matrix are stout, many climbers find this setup the most user friendly, especially when the second is slip-sliding and hanging all over the route. Under these circumstances, it's almost always better that the anchor (providing it is bomber) bears the loading, not the belayer's corpus.

A three-bolt anchor rigged for a **direct belay** (direct belay = belaying directly off the belay anchor) via a Petzl Grigri clipped into the power point. Note how the power point is at an ergonomically friendly chest level, ideal for managing a direct belay. Beyond the Grigri, other popular auto-locking devices are the Petzl Reverso, and the Trango Cinch. Here, another direct belay option would include the Munter hitch on a large, pear-shaped locking carabiner.

Remember this: a direct belay is an easy and efficient means to belay the second or follower, but never should be used to belay the leader. Also, understand that with all direct belays, when the anchors are less than ideal, any loading bypasses the shock-absorbing qualities of the belayer's body, and places the entire load directly onto the anchors. Granted, toprope forces are generally moderate, but any force is a concern if you've wandered off route and get stuck belaying from mank. When the anchors are rock solid, however, a direct belay is a quick, efficient and comfortable way to bring up a second.

Also note how the leader has clipped directly into the bolt hangers, bypassing the trashy, hardware store quick-links.

Three bolt anchor rigged as a **re-directed** belay. Understand that with every re-directed belay, the load is almost doubled where the rope is re-directed through the anchor. Always a sketchy choice when the follower considerably outweighs the belayer; if not well braced for the loading, a sudden force greater than their body weight can slam the belayer into the wall. Re-directed belays add friction to the system, and when the belayer is equal to or bigger than the follower and the anchors are mint, this technique makes for smooth and fluid lowering if the second is climbing up to, then getting lowered off, an anchor.

Guides frequently use a rope-direct when the anchor is set back from the edge and they want to position themselves near the edge to eyeball their client. In this setup you run the rope through two biners at the anchor's power point, climb back down to the edge, then tie an overhand loop on the doubled bight of rope. This now serves as an extended power point, and the belayer is secured where he wants to be. Here a Grigri is used for a direct belay from the new power point.

This is an easy technique that is especially useful at one-pitch crags where you belay from the top and the anchors are often set back from the edge. The end of the rope is clipped to the power point of the anchor system with a figure eight on a bight. Find your belay position and tie another figure eight (which becomes an extended power point), then simply secure yourself with a locking biner to your belay loop, and rig a direct belay (with a separate locking biner) off the extended power point.

As always, downward forces will try to drag the belayer into a direct line beneath the anchor—which is exactly where you might end up if your stance is not adequate and the anchor is not directly behind you.

Anchor Test Results

The previous discussion of the cordelette, sliding X and equalette was invaluable, but yielded only theoretical results about the relative merits of these systems. To answer the fundamental questions raised in that discussion, we needed to generate some hard data. The aim of testing was to determine performance differences between the sliding X and the cordelette when both systems were subjected to the same dynamic load (as found in a real world fall). Since hundreds of thousands of climbers literally hang their lives off these systems on a weekly basis, such testing was clearly indispensable to both this manual and the climbing community at large.

On the recommendation of Kolin Powick, quality assurance manager at Black Diamond, the physical testing was conducted by Jim Ewing, research and development manager at Sterling Ropes. Ewing is both a world-class climber and an engineer with years of experience testing on Sterling's UIAA drop towers and computer assist gear, and he is widely considered the leading tester in the United States. The tests took weeks and many late nights to complete (upwards of 200 drop tests were performed) and went far in answering many long-standing questions about rigging systems.

Very much an ongoing team effort, Ewing's raw data was worked up by nationally recognized statistical experts (and climbers) Dr. Lawrence Hamilton and Dr. Callie Rennison. Lastly, the tests led to a discovery phase involving several new rigging strategies that were field tested and refined by professional guides Bob Gaines and Tom Cecil and others.

Test Parameters

In order to devise the most significant tests, we first had to determine what factors were most crucial to a team building and belaying off a real world anchor. This involved examining the following elements of the anchor chain.

1) The primary placements. Hundreds of such tests already exist on the strength of "this" bolt and "that" camming device. Further analyses could tell us little about the applied function of either the sliding X or the cordelette.

2) The connecting points. In other words, the biners that connect the cordelette and the sliding X to both the primary anchor placements and the power point. Again, we initially believed such testing would divulge little about performance differences per either rigging system—a belief we later revised.

3) Materials. Because previous testing indicated performance differences between old-style nylon and high-tensile-strength cord and webbing (Dyneema, Spectra, etc.), we decided to use a variety of commonly used materials for all testing.

4) Knots. Tests have shown the holding power of high-tensile cord is reduced once it is knotted (less so in nylon). However there is little if any real world evidence to suggest that the holding strength of a use-appropriate, properly tied knot—tied in any material—has ever caused anchor failure. Hence the issue of knots and knot strength was ruled out as being relevant to our testing.

5) Extension. Not an issue with the cordelette. And with limiter knots (always advised), the extension possibilities of the sliding X are reduced to mere inches. As Craig Connally has shown, providing there is flex and give in the system—as there normally is in a real world belay and a real world leader fall—it seemed unlikely that extension of mere inches can ever cause the "shock loading" we so frequently read about.

While the limited extension (as found in a sliding X with limiter knots) was considered a minor factor in determining performance differences between rigging systems, we had no lab data to determine the forces involved during this extension. Wrestling with this long-standing question, Jim conducted a battery of tests that strongly suggest short extension does not cause any increase in forces (load multiplication) beyond the initial load on the system prior to the failure of one primary anchor placement. This is a fascinating, involved and important subject that warrants further research.

6) Redundancy. In terms of a belay anchor, a redundant anchor is different than an anchor that is merely backed up. A redundant belay anchor implies that the forces generated in a leader fall will never fall on one piece of gear. With a backed up anchor, the force falls on a single primary anchor placement, and if that fails, the force then falls on a second placement, and if that fails, the force impacts a third placement—the dreaded "cascade" anchor failure. To avoid this cascade scenario and to enjoy functional redundancy in a belay anchor (to avoid loading on one piece of gear), impact forces must be spread or equalized over at least two primary placements. To determine how well any rigging system accomplishes such functional redundancy would therefore involve the issue of equalization.

7) Equalization. Equalization is the very quality for which the sliding X and the cordelette were designed, and are employed, to achieve. After the previous analysis it became clear that the most meaningful testing would determine how well or how poorly the sliding X (dynamically equalized system) and the cordelette (statically equalized system) delivered on their promise of equalization.

To contrast the functional equalization of the sliding X and the cordelette, we decided on the following test parameters:

- "Slow pull," static loading tests have limited bearing on real world sport and adventure climbing. Only drop tests, using actual climbing rope, could replicate the dynamic forces of a real world leader fall.

- A drop test equaling a real world factor 1 fall would be used during each and every test. Factor 1 forces represent a significant but not shattering fall. Such forces would plainly illustrate how well both the sliding X and the cordelette distributed the dynamic load (in our case) over two primary placements of an anchor. It is almost certain that a greater or lesser dynamic force (than that of a factor 1 fall) would not change the actual load-sharing ratios, and that from the ratios provided by the factor 1 tests, we could reliably extrapolate up or down.

The test rigging was set up as follows:

1. Pieces of cord and webbing tied in 140cm to 150cm loops were used as opposed to the more typical 600cm. This length of cord was used to simplify setup.

2. The dynamic load ("mass") was dropped on 10.2mm Sterling Kosmos lead rope.

3. All drops = fall factor 1 on 0.5m of rope (starting length) between figure eight knots.

4. Mass = 100 kg

Summary: Simply put, the first tests answered the following question: If we rigged a cordelette and a sliding X off the same anchors (in both vertical and horizontal configurations) and subjected the anchors to a controlled, dynamic fall of exactly the same length and force, what might the test data disclose in terms of how well the two rigging systems distributed the forces between the two anchor points? Here is what we found.

These tests provided two distinct pieces of information about the sliding X and the cordelette rigging systems. First, the results offer the average absolute "difference in force" or "difference in load" between the two legs of the anchor generated due to a factor 1 fall. In some cases, these differences are close to zero, meaning that each leg of the anchor receives about half of the force. In others, the differences are quite high, suggesting that one leg is experiencing a disproportionate amount of the force generated. Ideally we would like to see the force distributed equally between the two arms of the anchor.

Second, test results indicate how consistent or inconsistent these measured "differences in load/force" are across multiple tests. In some cases, repeated measures will produce very consistent results. In other cases, great variation in measurements of these differences will be noted, suggesting that the difference in load

HORIZONTAL ANCHOR SCENARIO—EQUAL LEGS

Distance between anchor attachment points = 30cm ± 1cm

Cordelette configuration

Length of legs = 70cm ± 1cm

Angle between legs ≈ 24°

Sliding X configuration

Length of legs = 70cm ± 1cm

Angle between legs ≈ 24°

VERTICAL CRACK SCENARIO—UNEQUAL LEGS

Distance between top and bottom anchor points = 45cm

Cordelette configuration

Length of long leg = 55cm ± 3cm

Length of short leg = 12cm ± 3cm

Angle between legs = 0°

Sliding X configuration

Length of long leg = 100cm ± 3cm

Length of short leg = 45cm ± 3cm

Angle between legs = 0°

created will vary greatly from fall to fall. It is preferable that a rigging system generate little variation, or consistent differences in load measured, from fall to fall.

Systems Tested

A. Cordelette equal length: Tests simulating a factor 1 fall demonstrate that on average, a cordelette with equal-length arms configuration generated an absolute difference in load that was almost 1 kN (220 pounds), a significant amount. Repeated measurements of the difference in the forces generated varied somewhat across multiple tests. Contrary to conventional wisdom and popular usage, the cordelette, even with equal-length arms, is not a very effective system to achieve equalization.

B. Sliding X equal length: Testing of this anchor configuration shows that on average, the absolute difference in force transferred to each equal-length arm due to a factor 1 fall was very close to zero (i.e., about 0.2 kN difference). In other words, on average, there is almost no difference in load measured using a sliding X equal-length rigging configuration. This configuration equalizes very well. In addition, repeated testing demonstrates that the difference in force generated between the arms was very consistent across multiple tests. In fact, the consistency in equalization from drop to drop did not get better than this configuration. When compared to the cordelette equal rig, it is clear that the sliding X equal-length performs far better. Not only does the sliding X equal-length system equalize much better than the cordelette in a similar situation, it equalizes much more consistently from fall to fall.

How do these configurations compare in a situation in which one must build an anchor with unequal-length arms?

C. Cordelette unequal length: This clearly-the-worst-configuration tested produces an absolute average difference in force between the anchor arms of almost 3.5 kN, or roughly 780 pounds of force. Aside from generating the largest difference in force of the riggings measured, the cordelette unequal-length rigging was the most inconsistent when repeated measures of this difference were taken. In some cases, the difference in load measured was greater than 5 kN. To put it bluntly, the cordelette unequal-length configuration is the poorest performing anchor considered in all the testing conducted. Not only is equalization very poor, the degree of equalization varies wildly from fall to fall. This configuration is very unpredictable, except that the difference in the forces generated from a fall will be high. The cordelette unequal length is simply to be avoided.

D. Sliding X unequal length: The fourth configuration examined is the sliding X unequal-length anchor. This rigging produces, on average, an absolute difference in force between anchor arms of approximately 1 kN as a result of a factor 1 fall, putting it on par with the equalization obtained using a cordelette with equal arm lengths. Though the equalization offered by the sliding X unequal is on par with the cordelette equal, both are inferior to the sliding X equal. Of the two unequal-arm configurations examined, however, it is very clear that the sliding X unequal is the way to go.

In terms of consistency in equalization from test to test, the sliding X unequal-length configuration was as consistent in the absolute differences in load generated across repeated falls. Interestingly, though, while it tended to be very consistent across repeated measures, this anchor was also the most likely of all configurations to produce an occasional *extreme* difference in load. In other words, although tests showed this configuration to be generally consistent, it generated some unpredictably dreadful equalization.

Summary: This initial series of testing firmly establishes the sliding X as superior in terms of load distribution, while at the same time suggesting that the materials used played only a minor role. While the equal-armed cordelette distributes a dynamic load to an acceptable degree (barely), and will no doubt remain a viable option in that configuration, a cordelette rigged with unequal arms is an inferior—and likely hazardous—choice when contrasted with the more efficient load distribution of the sliding X.

The Sliding X—Why Unpredictable?

The sliding X with unequal arms showed acceptable but sometimes unpredictable loading. While still far superior to the cordelette with unequal arms, we wondered if switching out a gear component—mainly the power point biner—might produce more equal loading. This idea came from other tests that suggested the X was prone to binding on itself (the "clutch effect"), and that a wide-mouth, anodized biner could greatly reduce, if not eliminate, the clutch effect.

During testing Jim Ewing noticed that the X, or crossing of the cord or webbing, naturally wanted to settle right on the biner. In rigging the sliding X for this round of tests, he manually forced the crossing to occur on one or the other side of the biner in order to avoid the clutching effect (i.e., separated strands). He also used an anodized, wide-mouth (pear-shaped) biner for this set series of drops. To investigate the role of the clutch effect, additional tests were conducted. Pieces of cord and webbing tied in 140cm to 150cm loops were used, the dynamic load (100 kg) was dropped on 10.2 Sterling Kosmos lead rope and the drops equaled fall factor 1 on 0.5m of rope (starting length) between figure eight knots. In addition, the long leg equaled 100cm +/- 3cm, the short leg equaled 45cm +/- 3cm and the angle between legs equaled 0 degrees. Again, during tests, the strands of the anchor were manually separated on the biner. Here is what we found.

The sliding X unequal with an anodized wide-mouth biner produces, on average, a difference in force between anchor arms of approximately 0.5 kN as a result of a factor 1 fall. In other words, the equalization achieved using this configuration is better than that achieved using the sliding X unequal length (about 1 KN), and a bit worse than that obtained for the sliding X equal length (about 0.2 kN). Over repeated tests, differences in kN generated by this configuration varied at about the same degree produced by the sliding X equal-length configuration. This demonstrates that by removing the clutch effect, one can achieve equalization superior to that obtained using the sliding X unequal and remove the chance of an occasional lack of equalization.

While it's impractical in the field to separate the strands of the sliding X, doing so while adding a wide-mouth, anodized biner did result in near ideal equalization (basically 125 pounds of difference for a 1,500- to 2,000-pound dynamic load). This begged for yet another round of tests using the anodized biner, but not separating the strands of the sliding X. Yet in the process of reviewing the data and looking closely at the sliding X itself, it became obvious that the sticking point was the cross in the sling/cord, the actual X in the system. So long as limiter knots were used—as they always should be to limit extension—another option presented itself: Eliminate the X and simply clip two locking biners (with both "mouths" facing down and out) into the individual strands of the sling between the limiter knots. This rigging system was coined the "equalette."

To determine how the equalette compares to the sliding X and the cordelette unequal, a new round of testing was conducted. (Note: Because it is much more difficult to achieve equalization with an unequal-length arm configuration, testing focused on that mode.) Again, to maintain consistency, tests on the equalette were performed using pieces of cord and webbing tied in 140cm to 150cm loops, the dynamic load (100 kg) was dropped on 10.2 Sterling Kosmos lead rope and the drops equaled fall factor 1 on 0.5m of rope (starting length) between figure eight knots. In addition, the long leg equaled 100cm +/- 3cm, the short leg equaled 45cm +/- 3cm and the angle between legs equaled 0 degrees.

E. Equalette unequal length: The equalette unequal-length configuration outperforms the sliding X unequal-length configuration, and it performs as well as the sliding X unequal with a wide-mouth biner. Of course, unlike the sliding X unequal wide-mouth configuration, the equalette has the distinct advantage of being practical to use in the field. Equalization with unequal legs is difficult, and though the equalette did not equalize as well as the best-case scenario (sliding X with equal legs), it performs very well. In fact, the equalette offers the best equalization among the unequal-arm riggings considered.

Though the variation from test to test is greater for the equalette unequal compared to the sliding X unequal with a wide-mouth biner, the actual ability to equalize by the equalette is so far superior to the sliding X that it continues to be the best choice. In sum, this round of results shows that the equalette with unequal arms provides equalization equivalent to that seen in the sliding X equal-length rigging, and in instances when one requires an anchor with unequal arm lengths, the equalette performs significantly better than the traditional sliding X and vastly better than the unequal-length cordelette.

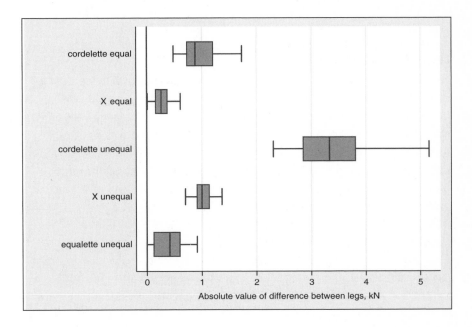

Note about the Quad

Extensive testing was also carried out on the "quad" system already described in this chapter. Since the quad is essentially a doubled equalette, and since tests on the quad revealed numbers virtually identical to the equalette, an illustrated argument about the quad was considered superfluous to this discussion.

Shock Loading

One of the longest ongoing debates (and one that largely, if not entirely, has been devoid of any test data) is the subject of "shock loading." Because this term has no meaningful definition, it usually is more confusing and misleading than informative. The conventional definition implies a force so sudden and terrific it could break biners and snap slings. The issue of extension in an anchor has always been a paramount concern to climbers, who feared such extension could cause this shock loading. When we looked to see what data had been generated to support this claim, we found none, and so we set out to conduct some preliminary tests.

Relevant to our discussion of rigging strategies, the key issue was what happens when one leg of a dynamically equalized system fails and the load falls to the remaining leg. Some have speculated that the load somehow multiplies between the time of the initial loading/arm failure, creating shock loading on the remaining leg.

As covered earlier in this book, all dynamically equalized anchors are only viable if they use limiter knots to limit possible extension. Given that these are in place, we wondered what the testing might divulge when one arm is allowed to fail and a dynamic load is sustained by the remaining arm. Here is how we went about the testing.

Leg-Failure Test of Equalette

This test used the same setup as previous unequal-leg tests but with the short leg connected with a "fuse." The fuse is meant to break before the long leg. We reused a sample of rope from earlier drop tests since a dynamic rope changes very little after multiple factor 1 drops, making the total force generated fairly consistent. Also, using the same piece of climbing rope greatly increased the chances of observing potential shock loading since after repeated drop testing the rope is only a little more dynamic than a piece of static line. If a shock load were ever going to happen, it would happen now.

It should be noted that when using a 100 kg mass and low-stretch rope, the forces are somewhat higher than one would expect with a fall factor of 1.

The drop tower computer program produces a force/time curve that is quite jagged immediately after the leg failure, indicating lots of vibration. It is obvious on the curve at what point the fuse fails. Immediately after the fuse blows, there is a sharp drop in force followed by the vibration, which is then followed by a normal-looking curve. The peak force varied depending on the tenacity of the fuse. The stronger the fuse, the lower the peak force on the remaining leg; the weaker the fuse, the higher the peak force on the remaining leg. Another interesting finding from these tests is that the sum of the force experienced by each anchor leg decreased as the fuse load is increased. In short, there is no "load multiplication" between the initial leg failure and the mass slamming onto the remaining anchor point. In other words, this series of testing demonstrates conclusively that *no cata-strophic shock loading* and *no "load multiplication"* occur as a result of the extension.

Shock-Loading Conclusion: In climbing systems, all the components have a degree of resiliency. These are by and large only maxed out when a section of unbelayed static line or high-tensile-strength cord sustains a dynamic load that is transmitted directly to the anchor, such as when a leader clips off to an anchor with a tech-cord daisy chain, climbs up 2 feet and slips, falling 4 feet directly onto the anchor. You can bust biners this way because the gear can't handle mass decelerating that quickly.

Stretch and give allow the mass to decelerate slower. In the daisy chain fall described above, you basically have the equivalent of a headon collision—something that's not going to happen when you're on a dynamic climbing rope that is running through a belay device, and when you're clipped into the anchor with the climbing rope. Here extension simply means that the next anchor that holds will be subjected to the initial load, minus what the first leg/piece absorbed. The load does not increase or multiply between the initial failure of a leg and the resultant loading on the remaining leg(s).

Materials

Testing so far has produced several important and some unexpected findings. Cordelettes by far do the poorest job of equalization. The sliding X equal and the equalette unequal are clearly the best configurations in terms of equalization. We wondered, however, what role was played by the sling materials used in the tests. We first looked at the cordelette. Here is what we learned.

The bars in the graphs represent the mean of the absolute difference between forces generated between the two arms of the anchor. In some cases, these bars are very small—close to zero—meaning that each arm of the anchor receives about half of the force generated by the fall (i.e., equalization). In other instances, the difference in forces transmitted to each arm is quite large, suggesting that one arm of the anchor is experiencing a disproportionate amount of the force generated. As was the case in earlier tests, we ideally would like to see the force distributed equally between the two arms of the anchor.

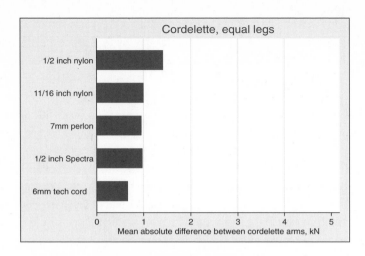

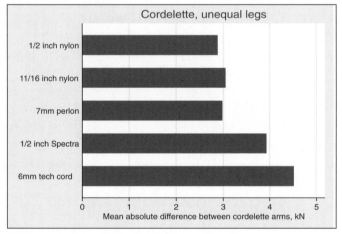

Considering the cordelette equal riggings, slight differences are noted among the sling materials, though substantively they appear to perform equally well. A different conclusion is reached when examining results from the cordelette unequal configuration. Findings show that nylon or Perlon provide better equalization than Spectra or high-tensile-strength cord, in the case of a cordelette with unequal legs. This suggests that for equalization purposes, nylon is the preferred material to make cordelettes. Though these results are based on limited data, it appears that for a cordelette unequal setup, *sling material does matter*.

Tests show much smaller differences in equalization across sling materials for the sliding X unequal and for the equalette unequal. In these configurations, sling material does not influence equalization greatly.

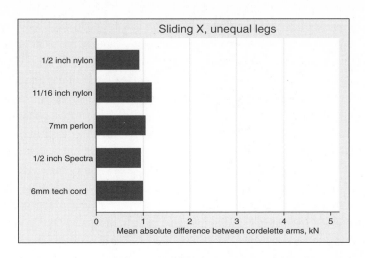

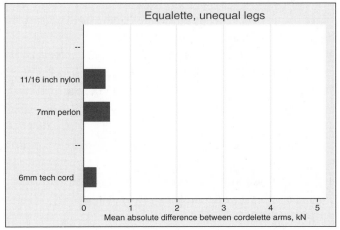

These findings reinforce what we concluded in the previous sections—that regardless of sling material, the cordelette is a terrible choice, the sliding X is a better choice and the equalette is the best choice of riggings tested for achieving equalization of two unequal legs. In addition, for use with two side-by-side primary anchors, the quad is also a handy system that provides easy use, brute strength and excellent equalization.

Summary

The Sterling tests were invaluable because they analyzed rigging systems, rather than equipment, and they applied dynamic loading (replicating the forces of a real world leader fall) on a dynamic rope, as opposed to "slow pull" or static loading on static ropes. Slow-pull, static-rope testing is a mode followed in many evaluations but one that has questionable relevance to real world climbing falls. Climbers do not lead on static ropes, and falls do not happen slowly.

Testing determined that unless a rigging system features perfectly equal-length arms and is used when the loading direction doesn't change so much as a single degree (and these are already imposing limitations), equalization and a fixed power point are mutually exclusive. The deduction is that future refinements in rigging systems will probably move away from fixed power points, with their big, beefy knots that, ironically, were long considered earmarks of security itself.

Some thirty years ago the sliding X introduced the concept of a sliding power point, and the refinements and tentative new systems spawned by the Sterling tests are the first baby step in taking the concept into the twenty-first century. Because this work is just beginning, I expect over the next few years to see many more options featuring a sliding power point. Simplified versions of the Trango Equalizer, as well as other "pulley" rigging systems, have already been presented and offer much hope for future innovation. No doubt others will devise new systems that feature strategies not yet imagined. A truly revolutionary method is yet to appear; we're basically still tweaking systems based on the cordelette and the sliding X. But no matter what the future turns up, it is doubtful that any single rigging strategy will prove "best" across the board. A combination of techniques will surely be required to cover the varied conditions found in real world rock climbing.

That much said, an obvious question remains unanswered: If the old systems— namely, the cordelette—tested so poorly in terms of equalization, why don't more cordelette-rigged anchors fail in the field? The answer is likely what we touched on earlier: Few belay anchors (no matter the rigging system employed) have ever failed because so few anchors ever experience a factor 2 fall. But for those very few teams that one day will experience such a fall—where the leader plunges directly onto the belay—we now have a much better idea of what actually works in terms of equalization.

It remains an engineering marvel that we can hand-place a collection of widgets into features in the rock and swiftly tie them off so the load gets somewhat evenly distributed throughout the matrix. No doubt we originally underestimated how tricky equalization was to achieve, largely settling for the cordelette on the strength of its apparent simplicity and utility. It came to pass that any other rigging strategy was judged by the simplicity of the cordelette (and other systems were generally found lacking), while all along the cordelette, if subjected to a dynamic load, was rarely performing as advertised.

Experience now shows that, in terms of rigging systems, the acronym KISS (Keep It Simple Stupid) is valuable only up to a point. We are free-soloing a slippery slope if we think the only rigging system worth using is one so facile that a rank beginner can arrange it with no training and no discrimination—a totally foolproof setup. In almost any potentially lethal endeavor, participants are required to learn the basic procedures to safeguard the adventure. Climbers simply have to master some essential protocols, and that's a fact. To expect rigging to be as simple as tying your shoes is to expect too much from the systems. Compared to what others learn—and must exercise—to fly a plane or scuba dive, climbers are obliged to know very little indeed. But it will never get to the point where climbers must know nothing at all.

All told, the Sterling tests are but one page in an ongoing investigation that will sire innovations as long as humankind is inclined to pull down on the Big Stone. A recent thread on rigging strategies featured on Rockclimbing.com received more than 35,000 views and generated 500-plus responses in fifteen days. Many ingenious rigging strategies were presented, and more are surely forthcoming. The bulk of these will come from grassroot sources for a simple reason: Rigging strategies are not products, and climbing companies only test what they sell. The gauntlet has been thrown down: Future rigging methods must be built on standard cord or webbing and cost no more than the cord or webbing itself. No doodads, widgets, rap rings or pricey sewing. Since there is little profit to a manufacturer in the simplified rigging methods most of us rely on, there's no motivation to develop or test such methods, even if the results are invaluable to real world climbers. It's up to us.

Climbers rappelling in the Needles, South Dakota. PHOTO BY BOB GAINES.

CHAPTER TEN

Other Anchors

TOPROPE ANCHORS

Toprope anchors must hold a load that is generally downward, though some side-ways pull may also occur. Forces on a toprope anchor never approach those possible on a belay anchor, but can reach 500 pounds or more due to the addition of weight from the belayer and dynamic loading in the system. When setting toprope anchors, keep in mind the following considerations:

- Evaluate any hazards at the site, especially loose rocks that the movement of a running rope could dislodge.

- Extend the anchors over the edge at the top of the cliff to prevent rope drag and damage. Professional guides prefer to rig this extension with a length of static rope. Pad any sharp edges at the lip. Make sure the rope sits directly above the climb, and make sure to run two independent strands of rope or webbing over the lip to maintain redundancy.

- Set the chocks and SLCDs fairly close together near the top of the climb when possible to reduce the number of slings and carabiners required.

- Avoid setting pieces behind detached blocks, flakes or other questionable rock features. Also, avoid having the rope near these features.

- Connect the rope to the anchors with two opposed carabiners, at least one of which is locking. If a spare locking carabiner isn't available, be sure the gates are opposed, and add a third carabiner. Climbing schools and outdoor programs routinely use three ovals opposed and reversed as their standard operating procedure, as do a growing number of recreational climbers. I have done my share of toproping, and whenever a locking carabiner is unavailable, I always triple the carabiners.

"Good enough" toprope anchor. The bolts are 5-piece Rawls installed with FIXE ring anchors. The high-tensile cord (4,000 pounds *single-loop strength* with triple fisherman's knot) is doubled then tied with a figure eight, leaving a four-loop power point. The rope is attached with three oval carabiners opposed and reversed. Clean, simple and strong. As discussed, any off-axis loading will put most or all of the force on one bolt, but in this situation it's extremely unlikely the anchor will fail.

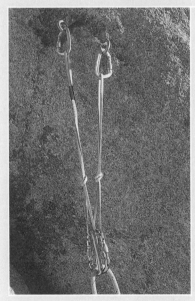

A two-bolt equalette rigged with webbing for an absolutely bomber toprope setup. Note how the gates are opposed and reversed on the carabiners. Owing to the sliding power point, this equalette can remain almost perfectly equalized between the two bolts, even if the direction of pull should change.

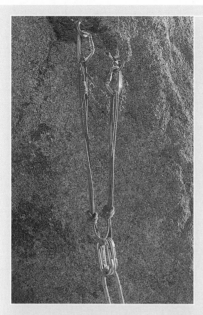

Two-bolt "quad" rig for toprope setup. Lab testing suggests that for two horizontally oriented anchor points (as shown here), the quad setup is basically indestructible. Field testing suggests that for those who frequently belay from, or toprope off, two horizontally oriented bolts (as found on top of countless sport and toprope climbs), a quad rig is your best friend. Simply keep it rigged (with the limiter knots tied) on a piece of 7mm nylon, or 5mm high-tensile cord, and break it out for use in these situations. Brute strength and fantastic equalization are achieved just as quickly as you can clip off the bolts and the power point.

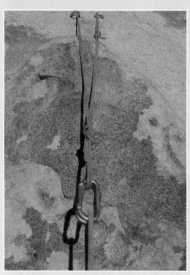

Simple two-bolt toprope anchor featuring a cordelette with two-loop power point. Rope is attached with two oval carabiners, opposed and reversed. The problem here is the way in which the carabiners rest right on an edge. This can cause the gates to open and create a dangerous situation. Always extend your toprope anchor over the lip of any such edges.

This toprope anchor consists of a 7mm nylon cordelette attached to two bolts with locking carabiners, pre-equalized with a figure eight on a bight and an overhand. The rope is attached with three ovals, opposed and reversed. The rope runs cleanly on this rig due to the fact that the power point has been extended beyond the lip. An extra figure eight knot has been added to shorten the rig and situate the power point exactly where desired.

- Belay toprope climbs from the ground whenever possible. It's more fun and easier to watch the climber, and far easier to micro-feather the belay if you can anticipate falls. (And falls should be expected. That's the very reason you rig a toprope in the first place.)

- Avoid belaying directly below the climber, in case rocks come off. Remember, though, that the force increases as you move away from the wall, or if the climber is built like Mike Tyson and you're a slender little chap.

- A ground anchor merely needs to provide extra ballast to help you counterweight the climber, so one bombproof piece is usually sufficient. Know, however, that the most common accident at Joshua Tree (one of America's most popular climbing areas) is a belayer accident, where the belayer is outweighed by the toproped climber, who falls and drags the belayer roughshod over uneven terrain.

- If you're in an exposed situation where getting yanked from your ground belay would be disastrous or even fatal, set up a redundant anchor system. Remember that an anchored belayer is a sitting duck for loose rocks, so don't lash yourself down in a shooting gallery.

Don't Be Nonchalant

Toprope anchors do pop on occasion. Several factors contribute. There's a nonchalant air about most toproping, since, in theory, it's a relatively harmless vocation. This nonchalance can spill over to the anchor setup. People can be impatient to get climbing and get lazy with the one thing that truly matters: the anchor. The most common danger is to trust old slings on a long-standing toprope anchor—clipping into the slings, rather than rigging a safe setup off the anchors themselves. Not good. When a toprope anchor fails, it's a very ugly affair. Generally there's a crowd at the bottom, eagerly waiting their turn. All eyes are on the present climber. He pops and splashes into the deck at your very feet. That can sour the sunniest day at the most enchanted crag. Take the extra time and rig it right.

The Ten-Point System

An increasing number of beginners are taught to create good-enough anchors through a standardized, criteria-based method called the Ten-Point System. Because beginners often toprope climbs, we present this system here. In basic form, it works like this: Hand-placed primary placements (nuts, cams, etc.) are assigned a score from one to four. A poor nut, for instance, receives a one; a decent cam that can hold much of its maximal load will be given a three; a no-doubt-about-it taper or hex in an ideal bottleneck placement likely gets the maximum four. The only primary placements that can earn five points are new bolts and natural anchors such as bombproof trees and blocks. After the anchors are set, SRENE is applied per the rigging, then you add up the score for the primary placements. If you attain a score of ten or more, your anchor is deemed good enough and no additional pieces are needed.

Of course, no criteria can perfectly guide a climber's judgment in awarding a score to a given placement, and one climber's "good enough" might rate only an eight or nine on another climber's scale. Nevertheless, the Ten-Point System has proven a very useful tool in teaching beginning climbers a sense of what is good enough, while casting doubt on most all two-piece anchors save those featuring bolts or burly natural features.

Here's a streamlined version of anchors that stand up to the Ten-Point System criteria:

* One tree;

* Two modern bolts; or

* Three solid pieces, *plus* one solid piece for an upward pull if you are building a belay anchor and any of the primary placements are not omnidirectional. (Solid means the piece alone would likely hold a worst-case scenario fall. If not, equalize it with an additional piece or pieces until the grouping meets the criteria.)

Clean and straightforward use of a static rope to extend a TR anchor over the edge. Both ends of the "V" have two camming devices statically equalized with cordelettes, tied with a figure eight on a bight on the left side and a clove hitch on the right side (for easy adjustability for the final equalization).

The primary placements are solid, secure and well equalized, but why not tie a limiter knot near the power point to limit extension? If you can determine the exact direction of pull/loading—and normally you can on any toprope setup—there is little to gain by using the sliding X. And in this case there's no redundancy at the webbing. All this anchor needs is a limiter knot at the power point and then you'd have it: Solid, Redundant, Equalized, and No Extension.

Same TR anchor as in the previous photo, but here the anchors are tied off with pre-equalized slings and joined with a cordelette. Providing the direction of pull is straight down, and it is on this toprope route, such a setup is superior to the set up in the previous photo, with its sliding X. The point is, you need not worry as much about building a multidirectional anchor when the direction of possible loading is only in one direction.

RAPPEL ANCHORS

Perhaps the most gruesome of all climbing stories is the case of the climber, high on a big wall, rappelling back down to a hanging bivouac after fixing a pitch. He raps off the end of the rope and windmills down into the void. Though this has happened, it is extremely rare. Far more frequent (though still very rare) is the case of the rappel anchor failing.

Rappelling is probably the most dangerous procedure in all of climbing, even though no actual climbing is involved. For this reason extreme caution should always be paid to every rappel, particularly toward the anchor.

Rappelling forces you to rely completely on your equipment and anchors. Walking is usually the safest mode of descent, but rappelling may be necessary, or more convenient. Don't take any chances with your rappel anchors—they must also conform to the SRENE concept. Check the integrity of existing anchors. Sometimes rats or other varmints will chew on fixed webbing, so check the entire length of any existing slings in the system. Also, aluminum rappel rings can be worn through, especially in soft sandstone areas (sand gets in ropes and abrades the aluminum ring). Always inspect the rings, and back them up when possible. The rings can be backed up with a second ring, or just a loop of webbing that the rope

Two ⅜-inch bolts. The left bolt has a stainless steel hanger, then a steel quick link to a steel lap link through which the rope is threaded. The right bolt has a welded cold shut with chain. The tackle on this anchor is a witless medley of various hardware store fixtures, none of which are designed for climbing anchors. The equalization looks good, and the rope is threaded through two different points for redundancy. Most climbers are leery to trust *two* hardware store fixtures and would never trust just one (like a single lap link) as the quality of the metallurgy is poor. When you come across one of these rap anchors featuring a mishmash of rusting chains and queer doodads, an easy way to give yourself an extra margin of safety is simply to tie a loop of nylon webbing through both bolt hangers as a backup.

While the two lengths of rusty chain would offer redundancy, it is lost where it all comes down to that one, measly lap link of unknown origin and vintage. Why trust your life to an aging hardware store relic some skinflint bought for 79 cents? This chain rig was easily backed up by threading a length of 1-inch webbing through both bolt hangers and tying it with a water knot. Though serious, these hardware store horror shows are rarely fatal owing to the modest loads generated by rappelling. As belay anchors, such setups are truly widow makers.

Rap rings. Left to right: FIXE stainless steel (12,500 pounds), SMC aluminum (3,400 pounds), Ushba titanium (6,750 pounds).

RAPPEL ANCHORS

- Statistically, rappelling is one of the most dangerous procedures in all of climbing.

- Rappelling forces you to rely completely on your equipment and anchors/rigging.

- Simple and avoidable rigging failures, not displaced nuts, cams, etc., are statistically the highest cause of rappelling accidents.

- Never trust, and always thoroughly check, the integrity of fixed rappel anchors (especially the rigging), and back them up if necessary.

- Excepting huge trees and titanic natural features, at least two bombproof anchors should be established at rappel stations.

- Avoid the American triangle rigging system. Anchors should be rigged using equalized slings, or at least slings of equal length.

- Never run the rope around a chain connecting the anchors.

- *Double-check all connecting links (anchor placements/slings, slings/rope, rope/rappel device, rappel device/harness) before you start down.*

- Always rappel slowly and smoothly to keep a low, static load on the anchor.

passes through but doesn't load. Don't toprope off aluminum rappel rings, either—use a locking carabiner instead. Avoid the sloppy habit of trusting whatever fixed gear exists. Back up existing anchors if you have any question. Don't save a dollar and be a mother's lament.

At least two bombproof anchors should be established at rappel stations. Occasionally rappel anchors consist of a single tree or set of slings on a rock feature, but climbers should back up anchors whenever possible. Anchors should be rigged using equalized slings, or at least slings of equal length.

A triangular sling configuration, also called the American triangle, is sometimes seen when two fixed anchors are side by side—two bolts on a smooth wall, two pitons driven into a horizontal crack, etc. There probably is not a cliff in America that doesn't sport this configuration, most likely as a popular, fixed rappel point. Unless the anchors are turbo-bomber and the slings are brand new, tie the anchors off individually and rappel or belay from two or more slings, or equalize the force on them with the sliding X.

Never run the rope around a chain or sling connecting the anchors. If one of the anchors fails, the rope simply pulls through and you're finished. Never lower from anchors with the rope running through a nylon sling, or the rope may burn

The American "death" triangle is something of a myth when it comes to rappel anchors. The fear is that this setup multiplies the loading force by pulling the bolts together. Under body weight the angle of the sling, at both bolts, is about 90 degrees. This is poor engineering by any definition. But given that rap anchors basically sustain body-weight loads, the American triangle, though always a wretched rigging strategy, is by and large only deadly when rigged to abysmal primary anchors.

Now we're talking—much better than the American triangle. Here we have two slings, fed independently through each bolt, and two rap rings. With this narrow of an angle the load is distributed nearly 50/50 on the bolts.

Two 5-piece Rawl bolts installed with FIXE ring hangers. Such ring anchors are becoming more commonplace owing to brute strength, simple setup and fluid rope removal. Visually unobtrusive, the welded stainless rings are stronger than the hangers. Over time, however, the rings often show signs of wear—from people toproping and lowering directly off the rings, as well as from countless rappel ropes being pulled through the rings. Always inspect the rings for wear.

This two-bolt rap anchor is well engineered. All the components are stainless steel. Both bolts are 5-piece Rawls. The left one has a stainless steel FIXE hanger with stainless chain attached to a final quick link; the right bolt has a Petzl hanger with a quick link/welded stainless ring combo. The positioning of the bolts combined with the hardware rigging makes for a narrow angle of pull between the two bolts. Good to go.

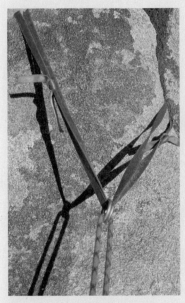

This setup is ideal save that the slings are too short and don't achieve enough coverage behind the top of the flake. If the rappeller should bounce or swing about during descent, the slings might shift on the anchor and slip off the left-hand, rounded edge of the flake.

That's what we're talking about. Two longer slings of 1-inch tubular nylon webbing tied with water knots, rigged with two rap rings. If you don't know the water knot, learn it (see the knots chapter). Many accidents have occurred with webbing rigged at anchors when some funky knot (something other than the water knot or double fisherman's) came untied. One knot that has failed in several instances (with fatal consequences) is the flat overhand, probably loosely tied and with no tail.

This sturdy granite rock horn looks bomber: well attached, thick and solid rock. However the tangle of old slings is stiff and degraded, the color faded from years in the sun. Worse is the fact that the sling is festooned with a single, hardware store quick link, providing no redundancy. If you find yourself on trad routes that may necessitate rappels from natural features such as trees and rock features, prepare yourself with a small knife, some spare nylon webbing and rap rings to re-rig old tat like this.

Old webbing, faded except where knot was tied. The sling on the left has the burn/melt mark from rope being pulled over it. Slings degraded by UV light will be faded and stiff. Worse yet is any sling with a slight rip or tear on its edge. Always replace such slings with newer material if you want to climb another day.

through the sling and deposit you on the deck fast as you can scream "Shiiiiit!" Rappelling with the rope running through slings is okay because the rope doesn't slide across the nylon slings when loaded, only when you pull to retrieve the ropes. Here a standard strategy is to clip a backup anchor into the main anchor so that when the main is weighted, the backup still has a few inches of slack in the sling. The biggest climber goes first, humping all the gear and testing the main anchor. If it holds, the second climber, who is lighter and gear free, removes the backup and raps off.

Smooth rappelling basically places a low, static load on the anchor. But when you start Ramboing down the cliffside in huge arcs, and especially when you slam on the brakes between bounds, the forces on the anchor can skyrocket. If the anchor is less than 10 ton strong, or even if it is, keep the forces low by trying to descend fluidly and light as a feather.

BIVOUAC ANCHORS

If you are bivouacked on a ledge, the main anchor is your principal security, though you often will slot a couple of regional nuts if you're sleeping at a distance from the anchor, or at a place where you can't easily tie-off taut to the main anchor (for instance, when the anchor is too far off to the side). Unless you're literally hanging over the edge, allow yourself enough slack so you can turn over in your bag, but not so much that you can roll off the ledge. Other considerations have to be worked out provisionally. It's mainly common sense.

Hanging bivouacs can get complicated, depending on the location and the number of climbers and bags you have along. Since portaledges came into vogue around 1980, the process has been greatly simplified. These are single-point sus-pension units, and most of the time climbers simply tier them one above the other. If you're all on a steep, sheer wall, it's simple—you just clip off to the haul line that is tied to the anchor. But if you're in a dihedral, or if the rock is peppered with roofs or other features, you might have to spread out horizontally. In these situations, most climbers will climb off to the side and place a provisional anchor or a rivet to actually sleep from, with the main anchor providing the real security. Whatever you're sleeping from, make sure it's bomber. If your bivy anchor fails, you're in for a horrifying plunge, and at least an hour of grievous cocking around to get things right.

One of the most jackass fads to ever sweep Yosemite Valley passed through in the early seventies. I don't know what blockhead conceived it, but for a while, at the time when wall climbing was the rage, it was the vogue to see just how meager an anchor you could hang from for the night. You were backed up by an absolutely bombproof anchor, of course, but what you actually were hanging from was as dicey as you were foolish.

Let me relate a few anecdotes to show how asinine this game was: There was talk once that the great Canadian wall climber Hugh Burton had slept hanging from a Leeper hook. It was twenty years later that he told me he hadn't slept, so scared was he to even wink, lest the hook pop and his reputation be ruined. For my own part, I can remember being halfway up a new line in the Sierras and slinging my

Scott Cosgrove hanging out on his portaledge, Higher Cathedral Spire, Yosemite, California. PHOTO BY BOB GAINES.

hammock from a number 1 Stopper. I was with Richard Harrison, who sleeps like Methuselah's father—deep and sound; but I've always slept like I was on deck for the gas chamber, more so when hanging from a harp string and squashed into a hammock designed for people skinny enough to shower inside a flagpole. Who could ever really saw some quality logs in those blasted hammocks, anyhow? Not me. And when later that sleepless night Richard farted, or a carabiner shifted, or something caused some such noise, I can promise you Lazarus didn't vault out of his sarcophagus any faster than I got the hell out of that hammock and onto the main anchor. That fad was a short-lived one.

BIG WALL ANCHORS

One of the difficulties in studying big wall anchors is in photographing them. Or trying to. On a genuine big wall, so much equipment (the bulk of which has little to do with the anchor) is on hand and the climbers are so close to the wall that getting a clear shot of the anchor is nearly impossible. We can replicate systems near the

Climbers on *Space Shot,* Zion National Park, Utah, one of the great big-wall destination climbing areas. PHOTO BY BOB GAINES.

ground, but they are not true representations of what you'll likely find on a wall.

The business of anchoring on big walls is a special study taken up in detail in *Big Walls!*, also in the How to Climb series. But understand this much: Big walls mean big loads, which means equalization is all the more important; and big wall anchors are complicated, requiring more time to rig, evaluate and to make sure things are as they should be.

REVIEW

No matter the particular anchor construct—bivouac, belay, toprope, rappel—the bottom line is that unless you make a habit of climbing on junk rock, or have a penchant for trashy routes, the majority of your anchors will be straightforward to rig and clean. In real world climbing it is rare that an experienced leader will yell down "Off belay" and not yell "On belay" within a few short minutes, the belay anchor rigged and inviolate. Keep it simple. Nine times out of ten, simplicity equals safety.

Experience will teach you much about building belay anchors. Always watch for innovative and slick setups other climbers may rig. You are never too old to learn a new trick, especially if it provides an easier, more straightforward method of dealing with an otherwise complicated setup. But no matter how simple the setup, always double-check your partner's work, watching for poor or sloppy anchors. Don't be afraid to insist on better anchors and more secure rigging if things look slipshod. Many climbers set sketchy anchors, and it's up to the rest of us to set them straight before the Four Horsemen gallop into view.

In closing let me reiterate that the anchor is the single most important part of the roped safety system, and that part of that anchor is the first placement off the belay, the Jesus Nut. But should the Jesus Nut fail, the anchor itself is your last line of defense. Remember the Golden Rule: The anchor must be able to sustain the greatest load conceivable in a given instance, or it is not good enough.

CONCLUSION

From choosing the individual placements, to rigging these into a power point, to securing the Jesus Nut directly off the belay, anchor-building choices are so varied they can stagger the novice and stall the veteran. With so many options, how can we be sure we're building good-enough anchors, or something less? We square off with that question on every belay, and one thing remains certain: without solid anchors, technical climbing is a swift way to die. The fact that total anchor failure happens so rarely—despite millions of climbers scaling millions of pitches a year—reassures us either that building secure anchors is routinely accomplished, or factor 2 falls onto the belay are extremely uncommon. And in those rare cases of catastrophic anchor failure, analyses suggest that the majority were avoidable.

WHEN OVERBUILDING IS NECESSARY

Several years ago, on the *Direct North Buttress* of Middle Cathedral (one of America's most fabled long free climbs), two strong climbers fell to their deaths, probably from the upper chimneys over 1,000 feet up the wall. Analyses of the rigging suggests a four-piece gear anchor ripped out, most likely from a factor 2 fall directly onto the belay. This alerts us there's a crucial call for anchors that would normally be considered "excessive" in cases where reliable Jesus Nuts are hard to find and where you could realistically take factor 2 falls onto the belay. Having made the fourth free ascent of the *Direct North Buttress*, and several forays onto the route later on, I recall many places where a leader is fortunate to arrange *any* protection 15 feet, or even 20 feet, off the belay. And up high, the belays themselves involve scratching around the back of grainy flares, looking for anything remotely sound. I mention this because such scenarios are not uncommon on the upper rungs of adventure climbing. Granted, by the time you get there you'll have considerable experience in building anchors. But as the tragedy on the *DNB* points out, the worst can befall the best of us. It cannot be overstated: Build every anchor for a worst-case scenario because some day you might experience one.

While initially puzzling and complex, mastering anchor-building fundamentals, and the ability to fashion variations on the themes, naturally comes with time and practice. Most experienced climbers can quickly tell if a given nut, cam or anchor is good or otherwise, just as a mason can tell at a glance if the bricks have been properly placed and mortared. Staying current with the literature, and taking an anchor seminar, can radically increase your learning curve and protection-placing/anchor-building competence. Every instructor will have favored ways of doing things, but the basic, field-tested principles will be the very ones we have covered in this book.

Can you always quickly and simply build an anchor? No. But you can and should strive toward simplicity and efficiency, avoiding needless slings, biners and garish setups. In many instances, the cordelette—even with its stated limitations—along with the sliding X and now the equalette, have streamlined the business of rigging, especially where the placements are spread around. And so long as you understand that a sound Jesus Nut placed directly off the belay is crucial to keep peak forces off the belay anchor itself, you are far along indeed.

In closing, let's return to a topic mentioned in the introduction: In the context of technical rock climbing, what does secure really mean? Or more importantly, what should it mean?

For some, security is an idea blind to the real life demands placed on climbers attempting to scale multipitch adventure climbs. On adventure routes from Col-

FOR THE LAST TIME . . .

Conforming an anchor to the letter of every sound principle does not guarantee that the anchor will hold a single pound. The best rigging can do no more than exploit the potential holding strength of the primary placements. Hence the first rule in building all anchors is to get sound primary placements. With bomber primary placements, the rules of thumb and modern rigging methods stack the odds in our favor that the anchor will do its job and do it well.

orado to Chamonix, time and equipment are variables that must be managed for a climbing team to consistently achieve success. On big routes, simplicity and efficiency—the Twin Pillars of this text—must extend beyond setting pro and building anchors, to the team's modus operandi. In alpine settings, where days are short and storms frequent, "speed equals safety" is a common refrain. When, in the name of safety, a climbing team wastes time and limited resources, at some place, on some route, the team will either have to bail or rush the process up high to compensate for time squandered below. And sometimes, the loss in time was due to building anchors that exceeded actual need.

The standard rationalization for over-building belay anchors is that an anchor is never too strong. An extreme view on this would consider ten bolts better than three. Here, appreciation for real world requirements gets clouded over by phobic engineering masquerading as safety. This view also fails to recognize that the top piece of protection always sustains the highest loading, and that the most critical job is to rig things so the topmost pro, and never the anchor itself, catches any and every fall.

As for belay anchors, there is good enough, then there is beyond good enough, the domain of the ideal, the perfect, the purely theoretical. Canadian climber Jeb Stillman recently put the subject into practical context: "Most of us try to construct anchors that somewhat exceed the standard of just barely good enough. Not by tons and miles, but by some acceptable margin that provides adequate peace of mind. Beyond building an anchor that will hold, most experienced climbers consider a couple possible what-ifs, then decide if it's worth the trouble of addressing them versus their actual likelihood and consequences. Every anchor I have built has been good enough. I'll admit that the margin has been tighter on a few, but clearly, every single one exceeded the threshold of good enough. Those of us who can't determine 'good enough' will naturally go overboard adding features that would, in theory, make the anchor better. But at some point, is it really? I mean, if the question is whether your anchor can hold one truck or three, one has to ask: Are you there to climb, or suspend trucks?"

That much said, efficiency is the last thing to come when learning to build anchors. In the early stages, the focus must remain on the absolute holding power and the security afforded by the rigging of your anchors, not on how fast you can build them or how much gear you can save in the process.

Before you truly know if your anchors are good enough or not, it's wise to build anchors strong enough to suspend two trucks, instead of one. Later if your ambition drives you up the rungs of adventure climbing, you will by that time have refined your technique to the point that you can settle for one truck anchor strength, which you can fashion simply and efficiently. And you will have to if you're ever to savor the spoils of adventure climbing.

At some time in your climbing career, be it one or twenty years into it, you'll seriously question why you are climbing at all. This is nothing less than squaring off with the Main Question of why are we alive, what are we doing, where are we going? The Main Question sneaks into the context of climbing because, well, because we're climbers. And every climber is on a voyage of discovery, no matter how unstated or unconscious the voyage might be. We can answer the Main Question with fancy opinions and second-hand beliefs. We might even throw the question back on itself, which is like telling God to ask somebody else. I reckon any meaningful response follows the requirements of building a solid anchor. In fact, your answer to the Main Question is your anchor in life, and in that sense your primary placements must be bombproof and the rigging simply and efficiently arranged. The noted chef Wolfgang Puck professed his own anchor matrix in a simple but telling motto: Live, Love, Eat. For many of us, it's Live, Love, and Climb. Perhaps the Main Question bubbles up when we temporarily misplace the first two placements in the matrix, or when we're belaying off only the third, instead of being equalized between all three. Everyone must answer the Main Question in their own way, but one thing remains the same for us all: To see this great voyage of discovery all the way through, we've got nothing if we don't have solid anchors.

We come to the cliffside to climb, and we build good-enough anchors and immediately slot that Jesus Nut, in order to safeguard our lives. Without a secure safety system, climbing is absurd. And without efficiency, climbing becomes a plodding, fear-based sham. Let us never forget that the safety system was devised to facilitate climbing. That's the name of the game.

Climb safely. Climb efficiently. Climb on.

Appendix

GEAR MANUFACTURERS AND SOURCES

Black Diamond Equipment, Ltd.
2084 East 3900 South
Salt Lake City, UT 84124
(801) 278–5533
www.bdel.com

Blue Water
209 Loworn Road
Carrollton, GA 30117
(770) 834–7515
www.bluewaterropes.com

Mammut Sports Group
(formerly Climb High)
135 Northside Drive
Shelburne, VT 05482
(802) 985–5056
www.mammutusa.com

Metolius Climbing
63189 Nels Anderson Road
Bend, OR 97701
(541) 382–7585
www.metoliusclimbing.com

Pigeon Mountain Industries (PMI)
P.O. Box 803
LaFayette, GA 30728
(800) 282–7673
www.pmirope.com

SMC
6930 Salashan Parkway
Ferndale, WA 98248
(360) 366–5532
www.smcgear.net

Wild Country
Meverill Road
Buxton, Derbyshire, England
SK17 8PY
44 (0) 1298–871–010
www.wildcountry.co.uk

Wild Country distributed in the
United States by:
Excalibur
P.O. Box 1007
Sandy, UT 84091
(801) 942–8471
xcalibur@mindspring.com

Yates Gear, Inc.
2608 Hartnell Avenue #6
Redding, CA 96002
(530) 222–4606
www.yatesgear.com

ESSENTIAL READING

Each year's climbing accidents are compiled and published in *Accidents in North American Mountaineering*, available at climbing shops nationwide.

Black Diamond comparative testing of high-tensile cord: www.xmission.com/~tmoyer/testing.

American Safe Climbing Association (ASCA) Web site, www.safeclimbing.org. Good resource for those who want to place bolts.

Supplemental Instruction

The American Mountain Guides Association (AMGA) is an excellent source of quali-fied instructors and guides. They can be reached at P.O. Box 1739, Boulder, CO 80306; (303) 271–0984.

Vertical Adventures, run by co-author Bob Gaines, offers instructional and guiding services in Joshua Tree and Idylwild, California. (800) 514–8785; www,vertical adventures.com; e-mail bgvertical@aol.com.

Index

About the Authors

John Long is the author of twenty-five books, with over one million copies in print. He is the principal author of the How to Rock Climb series. His short-form literary stories have been widely anthologized and translated into many languages. John won the 2006 Literary Award for excellence in alpine literature from the American Alpine Club.

PHOTO COURTESY OF JOHN LONG

PHOTO COURTESY OF BOB GAINES

Bob Gaines is an AMGA Certified Rock Guide who has been teaching rock climbing since 1983. He is the owner/director of Vertical Adventures Climbing School, based at Joshua Tree National Park, California, where he has taught clients ranging from Boy Scouts to Navy Seals. Bob has also worked extensively as a climbing stunt coordinator on over 40 television commercials. He was the chief safety officer for the movie *Cliffhanger* and doubled for Captain Kirk when Kirk free soloed El Capitan in *Star Trek V*. Bob is also the co-author of *Rock Climbing Tahquitz and Suicide Rocks* (The Globe Pequot Press, 2001).